ENDORSEMⱢ___ __

"In *Humanly Speaking*, Mike Spencer presents a compelling case for the humanity and dignity of the unborn and calls the church to respond accordingly. For the sake of precious children and hurting women, God's people should rise up to speak the truth in love. May God use this excellent book to empower church leaders and Christ-followers everywhere."

Randy Alcorn and Stephanie Anderson
Authors of *Pro-Choice or Pro-Life: Examining 15 Pro-Choice Claims—*
What Do Facts & Common Sense Tell Us?

"Reading *Humanly Speaking* will give you tremendous expert insights into the abortion debate. Mike Spencer speaks from a deep reservoir of experience and clear biblical conviction and delivers practical and persuasive tools gleaned from speaking to groups and one on one. He unpacks the core of this moral issue facing the church and graciously reveals how to champion the sanctity of human life faithfully and firmly."

Jor-El Godsey
President, Heartbeat International

"Mike Spencer is a master pro-life communicator, apologist, artful ambassador for the pro-life cause. Those virtues, alone, are reason enough for me to endorse him. But there is more. His character is deeply grounded in a love for Christ and the Church. I know, I worked closely with him for eight years. I recommend him to you wholeheartedly."

Scott Klusendorf
Founder and President, Life Training Institute

"Mike Spencer has written the definitive book on how the church should respond to legalized abortion. *Humanly Speaking* provides a clear, crisp, and incisive master handbook for pastors, church leaders, and layman who need answers pertaining to the greatest human rights violation of our time."

Mark Harrington
Founder and President, Created Equal

"There are far too few pastors speaking courageously into the culture in defense of the lives of pre-born children. It is the great moral tragedy of our day, and yet most choose to ignore the issue or speak on it only annually. Michael Spencer is a different sort of pastor, and *Humanly Speaking* is evidence of that. I wish there were more like him."

Jonathon Van Maren
Communications Director, Canadian Centre for Bio-Ethical Reform

"In *Humanly Speaking*, Mike Spencer offers a sound scientific defense for the unborn, but more importantly, he provides a clear answer to the profound question Jesus asked, 'Who is my neighbor?' Everyone–beginning with the unborn at conception–is our neighbor. If this is true, how should Christians and pastors respond to the greatest moral crisis of our time? After reading this book you won't be able to say you don't know. As a former pastor, Mike is uniquely equipped to offer guidance in a constructive way. It is my prayer that every Christian and pastor who reads this book will be moved by God's Spirit to act with grace and compassion, so together we might 'rescue those being led away to death' and 'hold back those staggering toward slaughter,' (Proverbs 24:11-12)."

Cathie Humbarger
Founder and Director of Public Policy, Reprotection, and former Executive Director, Allen County Right to Life

HUMANLY SPEAKING

The Evil of Abortion, the Silence of the Church, and the Grace of God

MICHAEL SPENCER

HUMANLY SPEAKING

The Evil of Abortion, the Silence of the Church, and the Grace of God

Michael Spencer

Print ISBN-13: 978-0-578-97493-4

Believers Book Services

2329 Farragut

Colorado Springs, CO 80907

Cover Design: Believers Book Services

Interior Layout: Ben Wolf (www.benwolf.com/editing-services)

Photo credit for copyright page:
Photo 5199484 © Slateriverproductions | Dreamstime.com

First Printing: 2021. Printed in The United States of America

To my wife, Barbara, who led me to Christ,
and to Christ, who led me to Barbara.

CONTENTS

OUR MANSLOW MOMENT

Manslow[1] was considered the class punching bag in my middle school back in 1975. I was in seventh grade, and Manslow was in eighth. As is the case in most middle schools, a sizable social chasm was fixed between these two grades. As a result, I didn't know Manslow very well. I did know that he was an unassuming, gentle-spirited, likable kid, although one to whom the awkward years had been particularly unkind. Overweight, socially awkward, and naive, Manslow spent his middle school years stuck in the crosshairs of heartless bullies.

One spring day, I ambled out of the school cafeteria onto the play-ground to find Manslow pinned to the chain link fence that served as the baseball diamond backstop. Two eighth-grade boys had spread his arms out and held his wrists tight against the fence, crucifixion style, while six or seven others had circled around to the back where they took turns running up to the fence and kicking it, jamming the fence hard into Manslow's body. This pubescent cruelty was like a scene out of William Golding's classic *Lord of the Flies*. Manslow felt every blow and begged for mercy but received none from his torturers.

Nor did he receive any from me. This was the first time in my young life I'd witnessed such violence. An uncomfortably warm, sick feeling washed over me, and my heart began to race. My conscience elbowed me to do something, but these were big eighth graders, and I was the runt of my seventh-grade class. I didn't stand a chance against them. I considered running back into the school and telling a teacher, but I feared retribution. And so, I did nothing. Manslow took his beating alone. It all happened quickly (though I'm sure this was not his perspective). In that moment, I joined the ranks of thousands of cowards before me who had assumed their unremarkable place in history as so-called innocent bystanders. To my knowledge, Manslow never knew I stood by and watched as he was treated so ruthlessly. But I knew and I was ashamed.

In His famous parable of the Good Samaritan, Jesus had something to say about those who sit by idly on the sidelines while others suffer. Interestingly, He chose a priest and a Levite—religious leaders —to make His point. And what was His point? Precisely this: the circle of moral responsibility for the Christian includes all people, regardless of skin color, gender, socio-economic status, or location.

I have shared Jesus' parable many times with teen and adult audiences. When I ask, "Who are the bad guys in this story?" the answer is always the same: "The priest and the Levite." Interestingly, rarely is the reply, "The robbers." I believe this is because our anger over their brutal act of violence is eclipsed by our disgust over the indifference and inaction of the religious leaders. We rightfully expect more. So does Jesus. In fact, He expects more from anyone who claims to be His disciple.

Legalized abortion presents the Church with our "Manslow moment." Like me on my middle school baseball field, scores of professing Christians, pastors, and priests are turning a blind eye to the unborn who find themselves stuck in the crosshairs of "choice." When well over 2,000 of the most vulnerable among us are being systematically killed every day in America, we should not deceive ourselves into thinking we can remain faithful to Christ on the sidelines. James made this clear: "Anyone, then, who knows the good he ought to do and doesn't do it, sins" (James 4:17).

I have often wished I could travel back in time to that moment at my middle school ball field. I'd do things differently. No, I don't think I could stop those boys from hurting Manslow, but I'd love another opportunity to try. I'd just like Manslow to know someone cared enough to share in his beating.

CHAPTER 1
EVERYONE HAS A BACKSTORY

I f someone had told me in high school I would one day become a
pastor, I would have died a thousand deaths. On my long list of
possible career choices, this one didn't even rank. Pastors were
boring, wore polyester, and spoke in a coded religious language that
seemed purposely designed to maintain their own irrelevance. This
was how I saw it, anyway. Yes, a thousand deaths would have been
preferable. But the pastorate is precisely where life took me. In fact, I
served in pastoral roles for twenty-three years and found tremendous
joy and satisfaction in my ministry. I love the Church and I loved
being a pastor. In 2012, I was invited to join the teaching staff of the
pro-life ministry, Life Training Institute, where I served for 8 years
before founding Project LifeVoice, a gospel-driven human rights
organization that equips and inspires pro-life ambassadors to speak
compellingly and to act sacrificially on behalf of our unborn neighbors targeted by abortion. Stepping away from pastoring was one of
the most difficult decisions I ever made. I didn't leave burned out,
bummed out, or pushed out. Nor did I leave with a messiah complex

thinking I was the answer to our national abortion crisis. I am one person with limited skills and abilities. However, I did leave with the conviction that practically speaking, the Church in America has largely abandoned the unborn. A small percentage of churches act in a manner consistent with the belief that abortion is a great moral evil and a lethal threat to children. It is clear to me that we will never convince those outside the church to stop aborting their children if we will not work to convince those in our own churches to stop aborting ours.

The subject of abortion is personal for me as I have been on both sides of the debate, and, to some extent, the abortion experience. Until 1984, I considered myself "pro-choice." Like many Americans, I knew abortion was wrong, but I viewed it as a necessary evil. Three personal encounters with abortion will help you understand my passage from supporting abortion to a commitment that every human being is equal before God and deserves to be cherished and legally protected from their earliest stage of development.

"I'M PREGNANT"

My first encounter with abortion took place in 1981. I was an aimless, self-indulgent eighteen-year-old dating a twenty-two-year-old woman I will call Amanda. I worked for her family who owned a small grocery store in the Detroit area. One evening, I was stocking shelves in the large walk-in cooler when Amanda walked in looking somber. Something was troubling her deeply. Nervously she blurted out, "I'm pregnant."

Her words hit me like a freight train. Thinking only of myself, I forcefully demanded, "You're getting an abortion!" Those exact words came out of my mouth. And they escaped my lips instinctively like the bark of a hungry, desperate dog protecting his bone.

Amanda cried but agreed to my demand.

The following day, before an appointment at an abortion clinic had been made, Amanda discovered that she was not pregnant, after all. By God's grace we were spared from a decision we would regret for the rest of our lives. Predictably, my relationship with Amanda eventually ended.

I have often reflected on my self-absorbed reaction to Amanda: "You're getting an abortion!" These were my words. I spoke them. They hung in the air like death. Jesus said, "By your words you will be condemned."[1] Indeed, my own words had condemned me. This story illustrates that there is little difference between me and those who've had abortions or have been responsible for them. I am confident that if Amanda had been pregnant, we would have aborted our child. Ultimately, it was not merely my words that indicted me; it was my selfish, darkened heart.

I thank God for His mercy and forgiveness in my life, but it is because of this experience that I sympathize with women and couples facing unplanned pregnancies, as well as with those who have made abortion decisions and now regret them. I am in no position to cast stones. The only difference between me and those who have had abortions is that for me there was no baby to abort. Not only am I in no position to cast stones, but I now feel compelled to do all that I can to persuade young mothers and fathers not to abort their children and to point those who have done so to Christ so that they might find forgiveness and healing.

THE SILENT SCREAM

The second encounter that shaped my thinking about abortion happened when I worked for a bank as a teller in 1983. It was there I met Barbara, who would later become my wife. Through her faithful example and witness, I surrendered my life to Jesus Christ on September 10 of that year. I was twenty-one and because of this decision, my life was about to change in ways I never could have imagined. The next morning, I began attending the church where Barbara's father served as the pastor. Within a few months, the youth pastor invited me to work as a volunteer with the teens. I gladly accepted.

Several months later, in 1984, I arrived at the youth meeting on a Wednesday evening unaware of the agenda. Forty or so students packed into the dank, crowded basement of the church parsonage to watch the newly released, groundbreaking film *The Silent Scream*[2] on a small TV set. Narrated by former abortionist Bernard Nathanson, the film shows an abortion being performed via ultrasound. I sat on one of the metal folding chairs that lined the back wall of the room with a direct view of the screen. On each side of me and on the floor in front of me was a sea of high school students serving as an impenetrable wall hemming me in. The next twenty-eight minutes became my personal hell as I witnessed, for the first time, what abortion does to a baby. I watched in horror and disbelief as a child was literally torn in pieces from her mother's womb. I don't know how this affected the others in the room that night, but the effect on me was profound. I have described this experience on numerous occasions to others, but always with a sense of defeat, never seeming to be able to convey just how deeply I was shaken. The parsonage basement had a walkout stairwell to the church parking lot. As I climbed those stairs to leave, I leaned briefly on the makeshift pipe railing, feeling extremely weak, and asked God to forgive me for the words I had spoken to Amanda a couple years earlier, and for believing abortion was anything less than evil. What I saw that night would change me forever and profoundly impact my future pastoral ministry and life direction.

ABORTION IN MY HANDS

Eight years later, in 1992, abortion became even more personal for me as I held an aborted child in my hands. Barbara and I were living in Fort Wayne, Indiana and I was working as a youth pastor. Fort Wayne was, and is, home to one of the most determined and effective pro-life communities in our nation. Through my involvement in that community, I met a man who had lifted a baby girl from a dumpster behind an abortion clinic in Detroit. She had been burned from her mother's womb at approximately five months of gestation by a poisonous saline solution. As I held her beautiful, perfectly formed but badly burned little body, the grisly reality of abortion touched me in a way that words cannot express—and in a way that even the imagery of *The Silent Scream* did not. I could hardly grasp the horror of it all. The little girl in my hands was dead with the approval of our Supreme Court, crushed under the heavy boot of "choice."

A good deal of my time is spent on high school and university campuses. I hear all the clichés and sloganeering of those who defend abortion, "Don't like abortion? Don't have one!" and "Every child a wanted child," etc. But these slogans disintegrate under the weight of a cold, lifeless little girl murdered by legalized abortion. When you hold a dead child in the palm of your hands, what remains to be argued? This precious little one had a backstory, too. But appallingly, hers ended with being tossed into a back-alley dumpster, left to rot like millions before her.

Let's not forget that the mother of the little girl whom I held in my hands also has a backstory, one that now includes ending the life of her perfectly formed daughter. I know from speaking with many people who've experienced abortion personally that the weight of this act is vastly more difficult to bear than the weight of the words I uttered years ago: "You're getting an abortion!" Our churches are filled with women and men who are haunted by past abortions. The Church's silence has sentenced many of these brothers and sisters to suffer alone.

These three encounters with abortion profoundly shaped my pastoral ministry and now shape my work equipping pro-life ambassadors in churches and schools, and at banquets and conferences, to make the case for life in a winsome and compelling manner. It is my joy to give voice to the little ones whose lives hang in the balance and to bring hope to young mothers and fathers who feel cornered by life's circumstances.

A CRUCIAL QUESTION

These backstories raise an important question. Is it possible for the Church to be a thunderous, protective voice for the unborn threatened by abortion while at the same time a grace-extending community for those who have had abortions or been responsible for them? The answer is an emphatic *yes*; that is, if we truly believe the gospel we claim to believe.

But before we go any further, I want to say two things that I hope will carry you through the coming pages.

First, I want to communicate my goals for this book. I hope to:

- Make the case for the dignity and inestimable worth of our tiniest neighbors, erasing the destructive invisible line of demarcation which has effectively created two classes of human beings within the Church: those we value and protect, and those we regard as unworthy of our gospel influence and ignore.
- Help you see your response to abortion as a gospel issue by bringing clarity to the role of the Church in an abortion-

supportive culture and by weighing the Church's current deficient response to abortion against the bright light of God's Word.

- Equip you to refute with confidence the lies pushed and peddled by our academic institutions, media, and entertainment industry related to science and morality, and prepare you to respond to popular challenges and accusations from abortion supporters, and embarrassingly, from some of our own brothers and sisters in Christ.
- Encourage pastors to act courageously and to "Be shepherds of God's flock that is under your care . . . not because you must, but because you are willing . . ."[3] by giving voice to the unborn and equipping your flocks to do the same.
- Point those struggling with guilt over past abortion experiences to Jesus Christ, the One who died to forgive each of us, and who promises to heal the brokenhearted and restore us to wholeness and kingdom usefulness.

Second, I realize you have your own backstory. We all have unconfessed, or at least unpublicized, sin. Just as I regret my words to Amanda, perhaps you have memories that trouble you. Maybe you have had an abortion or are responsible for one. Or maybe you are a pastor who has been reticent to speak and act on behalf of the unborn. Let me encourage you. As Christians, there is a sense in which each of us has lived two lives: the life we lived before we knew Christ and the one we now live in Him. And while the moment of salvation and justification for those who confess Jesus as Savior and Lord is powerful and definitive, the timeline delineating our old life from our new life is sometimes blurred. Even after coming to Christ, we sometimes act in ways we later regret. Thankfully, our heavenly Father provides a way of escape from our guilt and shame. This way of escape is through the Cross. The good news of the gospel is offered to the penitent unbeliever and the penitent believer alike. God's grace which has been made available through Christ's atoning sacrifice is sufficient for those who have chosen to abort their children, for the abortionist, and for the Christian who has stood by silently as these acts were committed. Christ promises forgiveness and freedom from sin: "Come to me, all you who are weary and burdened, and I will give you rest. Take my yoke upon you and learn from me, for I am gentle and humble in heart, and you will find rest for your souls."[4]

Like Christ, I also want to be both gracious and grace-extending. Although the subject of this book is heavy and at times burdensome, I have no desire to be harsh or uncharitable; my only desire is to be found faithful in the task I have chosen, or that has chosen me. Recognizing my own sinfulness, I want to be merciful to you, my brothers, and sisters, as well as to those of you who do not yet believe. I am guided by Jude's admonition; "Be merciful to those who doubt; save others by snatching them from the fire; to others show mercy, mixed with fear . . ."[5]

Having stated this, I am equally concerned about the interests of the unborn, whose interests are seldom of concern to so many in the Church. A critical analysis of the Church's ineffectual response to abortion, coupled with a challenge to speak boldly and to act selflessly on behalf of her womb-dwelling neighbors requires us to confront painful realities. Responding rightly to abortion requires us to think rightly about abortion. For this reason, I have written frankly, and at times uncomfortably, of the gruesome nature of abortion.

In addition, I have not refrained from writing candidly and critically of the unbiblical attitudes and paltry excuses employed by many pastors and professing Christians in their attempt to rationalize their lack of compassion for their most vulnerable neighbors. Such honest and descriptive language may offend the sensitivities of some of my readers. I would simply point out that a weak, feckless response to legalized abortion would do little, if anything, to contribute to its demise and would only add greater insult and injury to abortion's victims. The last five decades have proven this point.

Dietrich Bonhoeffer, pastor, theologian, and a key founding member of the Confessing Church in Germany, said it well and lived it even better: "We are not to simply bandage the wounds of victims beneath the wheels of injustice, we are to drive a spoke into the wheel itself."[6]

May God use my imperfect words to this hopeful end.

CHAPTER 2
RESCUERS, REFORMERS, AND CAGE-RATTLERS

B ritish writer and thinker G.K. Chesterton famously wrote, "Truth, of course, must of necessity be stranger than fiction, for we have made fiction to suit ourselves."[1] This is an interesting point. Hollywood's fictional heroes and villains are custom-made-to-order for us, the consumers. They look and act as we wish them to. Although occasionally genuinely entertaining, these invented figures are often predictably dull. But for good or bad, a quick trip through the aisles of Wal-Mart or to one's family reunion can dredge up some strange, real-life characters who are anything but boring, and who would easily validate Chesterton's claim.

But not only is truth stranger than fiction, sometimes it is much more inspiring. The catalogue of thousands of years of church history provides ample evidence to this effect. The Old and New Testaments, *Foxe's Book of Martyrs*, and hundreds of other historical accounts present us with real-life heroes, imperfect people, sometimes seriously flawed in character, but whose valiant acts of faith nonetheless changed the course of history. Indeed, our family tree is home to many godly rescuers, reformers, and cage-rattlers, most of whom served and sacrificed without fanfare and without notice, often paying with their own blood for the privilege of bettering our world. Many of their names have been all but forgotten, and yet their godly influence lives on. This is just one of the reasons why I love the Church.

But my love for the Church is also borne out of personal experience. One of my earliest encounters with the Church happened when I was eleven years old. My dad had just come to faith in Christ and began attending a small Baptist church which I visited a handful of times. The congregation had converted a house into a meeting place: they tore out walls, brought in pews, and began holding worship services. This small, loving band of Christ-followers ran a ministry to those who were hearing-impaired and unable to speak. Some of them would occasionally tap my arm and utter inaudible sounds to get my attention. I remember the awkwardness of not knowing how to respond. As socially uncomfortable as this was, it struck me that these people would have been mocked and ostracized in my school, but here they were loved and accepted.

Years later, after coming to faith in Christ and attending the church Barbara's father pastored, I couldn't help but notice that this church displayed the same kind of selfless and unconditional love. They routinely reached out to the developmentally challenged, the homeless, single moms, and many others too often overlooked by the rest of society. No longer archaic and boring, as I had previously thought, I was now enthralled with and falling in love with the Church. Whereas before I had viewed all pastors as out of touch and self-serving, I was now being influenced by pastors who joyfully sacrificed their own comfort to meet the needs of others.

My family has frequently been on the receiving end of our local church's rich generosity. In 2001, I was diagnosed with stage 4 cancer. The prognosis was not good. Barbara and I had four young children at the time and our lives were about to be turned upside down by surgeries, chemotherapy, and radiation. As a result of these treatments, my body became severely weakened and I was unable to work for an entire year. But with the help of our local church, all our bills were paid. In addition, the men of our church provided lawncare, and the women brought in meals. On multiple occasions, families from our church entertained our children in their homes and took them shopping and to various social events. One brother from another church walked door-to-door in his neighborhood in the rain to ask for donations for my family. We wept when he delivered an envelope stuffed full of cash to our home.

Yes, I love the Church and I am in good company. Jesus loves the Church so much that He "gave Himself up for her"[2] by becoming "obedient unto death, even death on a cross."[3] In stark contrast to the widespread disdain many Americans have for the Church, Jesus, ever the perfect and faithful husband, loves His bride deeply and passionately. Despite her many shortcomings and imperfections, no other religious institution, business, or charitable group loves and serves like the Church.

CHRISTIANITY: A THREAT TO CIVILIZATION?

Increasingly, the Church in America is mocked and criticized. Christians are consistently portrayed in movies, in the media, and on university campuses as self-righteous, judgmental, and even hateful. The blood red capes and white bonnets of Hulu's TV series *The Handmaid's Tale* have become the protest attire for many on the political left who wish to depict Christian men as misogynistic, repressive devils who use women for surrogate sexual slavery. In addition, many of our detractors have convinced themselves that the Church is full of hypocrites. They love to declare their abhorrence of organized religion, apparently preferring the disorganized religion of atheism. Many atheists, such as Lawrence Krauss, Richard Dawkins, and Sam Harris portray the Church not merely as fossilized or obsolete, but as dangerous—a menacing threat to democracy and to civilization itself. In addition, we are routinely depicted in the public square as unthinking "science-deniers."

This less-than-charitable spirit toward the Church shouldn't surprise us. Jesus told the disciples, "If the world hates you, keep in mind it hated me first."[4] But what is particularly troubling is that it is not just atheists and those outside of the Church who launch bitter salvos against her. Much of the criticism and denunciation of the Church comes from those within our own ranks. Sadly, many Christians today find themselves in the grip of a self-loathing spirit, apparently fueled by the foolish and naive notion that by constantly berating ourselves we might somehow appease our enemies and cause them to like us, or to at least leave us alone. Of course, this approach does nothing to placate our antagonists and only further embitters and emboldens them toward us. It also does nothing to instill within our children a love for the Church that Christ loves so deeply.

This negative attitude reinforces the wildly unfair and damaging stereotype our foes have created for us while conveniently ignoring the positive sanctifying influence of the Church in American culture and throughout the world. Now admittedly, the weakened, and at times, apostate condition of many American churches is a scandal to the name of Christ and a great embarrassment to us. The Church's sins and failures are many, and the black eye this has visited upon our gospel witness is largely self-inflicted. The Church must own up to her failures and invite greater accountability. But we should also be quick to champion the undeniably positive influence of the Church throughout the world because when it comes to loving the oppressed, the marginalized, and those unjustly sentenced to death, no one does it better. For all her faults, there is still nothing like the radiant bride of Jesus Christ.

In a passage commonly known as "Peter's Great Confession,"[5] Jesus confronts Peter with a question that has divided nations and households for centuries: "Who do the people say the Son of Man is?" Peter responds, "Some say John the Baptist; others say Elijah; and still others Jeremiah or one of the prophets." Jesus then asks, "But what about you? Who do you say I am?" Peter's answer was inspired: "You are the Christ, the Son of the living God." At this point, Jesus shifted the attention from Himself onto Peter and the other disciples with a declaration that gives us an important glimpse at His divine purpose for the Church: "And I tell you that you are Peter, and on this rock, I will build my Church and the gates of Hades will not overcome it." The picture Jesus paints of the Church is not that of a spiritually anemic, antiquated institution of a bygone era, but of an invincible, advancing, and triumphant army created and called by God to kick in the gates of hell.

GENTLE WARRIORS

No, we are not militants. Rather, we are a band of gentle warriors, compelled by Christ's love and by the humility that characterizes those who have been forgiven a great debt, to take the gospel to the ends of the earth, to bind up the wounds of the broken-hearted, and to rescue those being led away to death. And we don't cut the heads off our enemies. Instead, we love and pray for them. By doing these things and so much more, we steamroll over hell's gates.[6]

We are individuals from every race, tongue, tribe, and social class bound together throughout history by a simple yet common confession: that apart from the atoning sacrifice of our Lord and Savior, Jesus Christ, we are morally doomed sinners without hope. We are in no position to look down on anyone, for we, too, were once God's enemies. But by God's grace, Jesus now calls us His friends.[7]

Armed with the gospel of Jesus Christ and a sacrificial love for others, the Church is the hope of the world. If you have placed your trust in Jesus Christ for forgiveness and salvation, then you are part of this great hope.

Christianity has proved a powerful force for good wherever the gospel has been exported. We establish hospitals, universities, soup kitchens, rescue missions, food banks, women's shelters, orphanages, and adoption agencies. We drill wells in Africa and Asia, and we rush to every catastrophe around the world to help. We advocate for those caught in the jaws of sex-trafficking, and we minister to those struggling with addictions. And contrary to popular belief, we adopt and foster children at a disproportionately higher rate than non-Christians. Barna reports that 5 percent of practicing Christians in the United States have adopted children; more than twice the number of all others who have adopted. In addition, 3 percent of Christians, compared to only 2 percent of all U. S. adults are foster parents.[8] This is a stunning statistic when one considers that the 2 percent includes adults of all other religious backgrounds combined–Muslim, Jewish, Buddhist, etc. The fact is, the foster care system in the United States, as imperfect as it may be, would nonetheless collapse in on itself if not for the thousands of Christian families who have opened their hearts and homes to children in need.

Furthermore, who can deny that slavery in England and in America were ended because of the fiery opposition of Christians like William Wilberforce, William Lloyd Garrison, and Harriet Tubman?

THE PYGMY IN THE ZOO

In the book *Ota Benga: The Pygmy in the Zoo*, authors Phillips

Verner Bradford and Harvey Blume recount the painful life story of Ota Benga, a young pygmy from the Congo who became the main attraction in an anthropology exhibit at the Louisiana Purchase Exposition in St. Louis, Missouri in 1904, and later in a disgraceful "human zoo" exhibit in 1906 at the Bronx Zoo. Ota had been freed from African slave traders by Samuel Phillips Verner, an entrepreneur recruiting Africans for the Exposition, and eventually traveled with Verner to the United States. At the Bronx Zoo, Ota was free to roam the grounds, but only before and after he was "exhibited" in the zoo's Monkey House each day.

Exhibits of humans with black and brown skin were presented as examples of earlier stages of human evolution and became quite popular in the early twentieth century, as Darwin's theory of natural selection began to take hold. As a result, thousands of curious spectators flocked to see the little black man who stood only four feet, eleven inches and weighed 103 pounds.

It was Christians–pastors in particular–who opposed Ota's mistreatment as a lesser human and fought for his freedom. At one point in this struggle, a black pastor named James H. Gordon declared, "Our race, we think, is depressed enough, without exhibiting one of us with the apes . . . We think we are worthy of being considered human beings, with souls."[9] Dr. R.S. MacArthur, the spokesman for a delegation of black churches, petitioned the mayor of New York City for his release from the zoo. As a result, Ota was eventually released to Pastor Gordon, who ran the Howard Colored Orphan Asylum in Brooklyn, and made him a ward. This afforded Ota the chance to indulge his voracious appetite for learning. He was tutored in English and eventually took on employment. Ota longed to return to his home in Africa, but the outbreak of World War I prevented him from doing so, plunging him into a deep depression and resulting in his tragic suicide at only thirty-two years of age.

Today his body is buried in an unmarked grave in Lynchburg,
Virginia.

THE SOUL OF LE CHAMBON

Consider the Christian example of Pastor André Trocmé who
pastored a remote parish in Le Chambon-sur-Lignon, a small village
in south-central France. Pastor Trocmé had been sent there because of
his pacifist convictions which were at odds with the French Protestant
Church. Nonetheless, Pastor Trocmé bloomed where he had been
planted. He spoke out bravely from his pulpit against discrimination
as the Nazis continued to gain power in neighboring Germany. He
frequently admonished his flock to "do the will of God, not of men"
and when Jewish deportations began in France in 1942, he urged his
flock to give shelter to "the people of the Bible."

Under his courageous pastoral leadership, the entire community
became a well-oiled rescue operation for Jews fleeing the Nazis and
their French collaborators. The village and outlying areas were soon
populated with hundreds of Jews seeking shelter. It is estimated that
over a five-year period at least 3,500 Jewish men, women, and children found safety there. Some were given permanent shelter, while
others were hidden on farms until they could escape across the border
to Switzerland.

Remarkably, no Chambonnais ever denounced or betrayed a
single refugee. However, the Vichy authorities eventually became
suspicious of Pastor Trocmé. A warrant for his arrest was issued and
in February of 1943 he was apprehended and sent to an internment
camp along with two others. When asked where the Jews were
hiding, he responded, "I don't know what a Jew is. I only know a
man." When his captors angrily demanded he cease his rescue activities, Trocmé responded, "These people came here for help and for

shelter. I am their shepherd. A shepherd does not forsake his flock."[10]

Pressured to sign a commitment to obey all government orders, Pastor Trocmé refused to do so. Nevertheless, he was released but was forced underground where he continued his rescue efforts. Today, nearly 80 years later, Pastor André Trocmé is known as "The Soul of le Chambon."

OUR CONSUMMATE RESCUER

Throughout history, whenever injustice is found, whenever poverty or racism abounds, whenever the weak and vulnerable are caged or hunted like animals, faithful Christians like Pastor Trocmé become rescuers, often at great personal cost. There is a reason for this: Our Lord, Jesus Christ, is the consummate rescuer. "We love because He first loved us."[11]

In Hebrews 11:32-34, we read of Gideon, Barak, Samson, Jephthah, David, Samuel, and the prophets, who, through faith, conquered kingdoms, shut the mouths of lions, quenched the fury of the flame, and (notice these words) *administered justice*. Taming lions and administering justice has always been the work of the Church.

The widespread pagan practice of infant abandonment was both legal and common in first century Rome. Newborns were abandoned for nearly any reason and without legal penalty or social stigma. But Jesus's followers rescued these unfortunates, taking them into their homes. And while the masses fled diseased and plague-ridden cities to save their own skin, Christians stayed and served. These stories are inspiring and convicting, but they come as no surprise; God's Word frequently commands us to love all men sacrificially and to lay down our lives for one another.

For thousands of years Christ's arms of love have been reaching into the darkest and most forsaken corners of the world–into leper communities, penal colonies, the garbage dumps of Mexico City, the slums of Mumbai, and our own inner cities. His hands continue to heal, and His feet continue to go as the Church marches on in her centuries-long commitment to love a world besmirched by sin and its malignant effects.

FABRICATED INDIGNATION

The racially motivated exploitation of Ota Benga is a disgraceful event in our nation's history. Today, almost every apparent form of bigotry is condemned in the strongest possible terms.

However, it seems much of this expressed indignation is fabricated since the same thinking that once put Ota into the Monkey House now puts the unborn into incinerators and dumpsters—and this with the vehement support of many of today's "tolerant" moralists who wag their fingers condemningly at the Church and protect the shedding of innocent human blood for profit. They congratulate themselves for having moved beyond the moral ignorance of Ota's captors who viewed him as a lesser human simply because of his size and skin color while they defend the destruction of unborn children simply because of their size, sex, or location. This is hardly a picture of tolerance.

There is no denying it: the worldview of secular humanism put a man in a cage, but the Christian worldview let him out. Yes, it was Christianity that produced the outspoken Pastor James H. Gordon who stood on the shoulders of the Hebrew midwives, who centuries earlier, disobeyed Pharaoh's order to murder every newborn Hebrew boy. Countless other examples of Christian rescuers could be cited. What a rich legacy we have been given.

BUT SOMETHING HAS GONE TERRIBLY WRONG

It is precisely because our family tree is so heavily populated with selfless rescuers and reformers that the deafening silence of much of the Church with respect to abortion's helpless victims is so grievous and scandalous. It seems the boundaries for cultural engagement have been drawn, not by the dictates of God's Word, but by the brute forces of self-interest and political correctness, constricting our circle of moral responsibility so tightly as to exclude those who are most marginalized and oppressed, and most in need of our help: our unborn neighbors.

Tragically, for most Americans, even for most Christians, the word "abortion" has lost all meaning. For many, abortion isn't real; it is abstract, synthetic–even sanitary. As a result, most Christians have been afforded the "luxury" of indifference.

Few Christians have the fortitude to read the graphic details of abortion. Even fewer are willing to watch a video or look at photos of the victims. Abortion is horrific. It wrenches our guts and pains our hearts. But if we hope to see an end to legalized abortion, we must look. Winning the war against this lethal enemy requires us to look at the mangled and butchered bodies of little boys and girls who serve as the irrefutable evidence that the real extremists and those "waging a war on women" are not pro-lifers, but those who deny the unborn their most fundamental right: the right to continue living. Abortion is the intentional and unjust killing of innocent unborn human beings. This act is committed against them at their most vulnerable stage of development in the most barbaric manner imaginable. Abortion dismembers, decapitates, disembowels, or induces a heart attack by injecting digoxin or potassium chloride into the child's heart, killing her in her mother's womb. After she is violently extracted from her mother, she is then flushed, incinerated, or parted out for cash like a junked car to the highest bidder.[12] Refusing to look at abortion's victims allows those who defend abortion as well as those whose pro-life convictions are paper thin to sleep comfortably, never having to wrestle with the unpleasantness of dismembered limbs, crushed skulls, and burned bodies.

I frequently encounter devoted pro-lifers who have become jaded by the Church's silence over abortion. Having concluded that any effort to arouse the Church's passion for the unborn is a fool's errand, many have become disillusioned and have given up on the Church altogether. I share their frustration. But the unborn need the Church's voice, which means the Church needs ours. Called to be God's standard-bearer and to lead in this struggle for human dignity and equality, the Church is duty-bound to contend for the weak and needy, to look after orphans and widows, and to rescue those whose lives are imperiled by wicked men. If roused from her unholy slumber, she poses a formidable threat to this Philistine giant we call abortion. But if the Church will not be roused, she should at least be denied the luxury of easily avoiding our prophetic witness and sleeping comfortably as her own children cry out for her protective arms as they are led away to death.

Together we can change the world one unborn child at a time and thereby add our names to that long and glorious list of rescuers, reformers, and cage rattlers who are still changing the world for the glory of God.

CHAPTER 3
WHAT IS THE ZYGOTE AND WHY DOES IT MATTER?

The Bible leaves little room for confusion regarding our moral duty to our fellow human beings. In Leviticus 19:18, God commanded His people, "Love your neighbor as yourself." In this immediate context, "neighbor" referred primarily to their fellow Israelites. Just a few verses later, the definition of "neighbor" is expanded to include "the foreigner residing among you." But our ethical boundary line doesn't stop there. Centuries later, when a confused expert in the moral law asked Jesus, "And who is my neighbor?" Jesus answered with the much-loved parable of the Good Samaritan, further expanding the definition of "neighbor" to include anyone within our sphere of influence and even strangers who have been robbed, beaten, and abandoned in ditches.

IS THE EMBRYO MY NEIGHBOR?

The scourge of legalized abortion confronts us with a similar but narrower question: Is the zygote, or early embryo, my neighbor?

This is the moral question at the heart of the abortion debate, and one that cannot be properly answered without first answering the scientific question: is the zygote a human being or some other kind of being? In other words, when does a human begin to exist? For many people, even for many Christians, the suggestion that a single-cell zygote, smaller than a period at the end of a sentence, is a distinct, living, and whole human being with equal moral standing to the man in the ditch seems absurd. But intuitions can be wrong and looks can be deceiving. Thinking rightly about abortion requires us to think rightly about the nature of the zygote. This is the starting point for understanding the Church's role in an abortion-supportive culture.

To establish the proposition that the zygote is a full-fledged member of the human community is to argue that this same human being has a legitimate claim to be protected by laws that secure his or her right to live and flourish among us. But even if the state deprives the vulnerable zygote of this most fundamental human right, as it has, a solid layer of protection should be afforded these tiny humans by the Church. The abundance of Old and New Testament commands intended to safeguard human life and dignity would obligate us to shield such human prey–the youngest and most defenseless among us–from violent oppressors. Therefore, establishing the full humanity of the zygote as the earliest stage of a human being in its development is the first step in answering the moral question: is the zygote my neighbor?

When it comes to determining the moral status of the unborn, many abortion supporters suffer from an appalling lack of scientific curiosity. Disregarding the clear conclusions of embryologists, they would have us believe that no one knows when human life begins. Regarding that crucial question, our Supreme Court took this willful ignorance a step further, arguing that the question itself was trivial and the quest for an answer was futile. Writing the majority opinion in *Roe v. Wade*, Harry Blackmun stated,

> "We need not resolve the difficult question of when life begins. When those trained in the respective disciplines of medicine, philosophy, and theology are unable to arrive at any consensus, the judiciary, at this point in the development of man's knowledge, is not in a position to speculate as to the answer."[1]

Nineteen years later, in the 1992 Supreme Court decision *Planned Parenthood v. Casey*, Justice Anthony Kennedy saw things differently. He argued that an answer to the question could indeed be found, or more accurately, could be subjectively created by each individual. In this decision, Kennedy wrote what has aptly come to be known as the notorious "Mystery Passage." It reads, "At the heart of liberty is the right to define one's own concept of existence, of meaning, of the universe, and of the mystery of human life."[2]

Not surprising, nascent children are denied this supposed "right." Instead, they are victimized by the morally relativistic definitions that the powerful invent to justify aborting them. For instance, when former Planned Parenthood president Cecile Richards was asked during an interview when a human being becomes a human being, she answered, "I am the mother of three children. For me, life began when I delivered them."[3] This is a predictably convenient response from someone who presided over the world's largest abortion business for twelve years. Cecile's ideology forced her to abandon moral intuition and scientific evidence; to believe the ultrasound images she presumably saw of her own children and the kicks she most certainly felt bumping against her abdomen were nothing but the grainy pictures and primal movements of parasitic clumps of cells that miraculously became human beings at birth.

An objective understanding of our biological beginnings cannot be formulated by relying on subjective tests or wishful thinking. Richards' convenient and radically individualized approach to defining when human life begins flouts the fact that species membership is scientifically determined. It is not open to personal definitions or opinions.

While pro-lifers (and Christians in general) are routinely portrayed as "science deniers," the pro-life position is firmly established on the scientific facts of human embryology. And what do human embryologists tell us about the zygote? Doctor C. Ward Kischer, Emeritus Professor of Anatomy at the University of Arizona, states: "The life of the new individual human being begins at fertilization (conception). It is significant to state that every human embryologist, worldwide, knows this (it is not a belief), and it is so stated in virtually every textbook of human embryology."[4] Respected embryologists Keith L. Moore, T.V.N. Persaud, and Mark Torchia, concur: "A zygote is the beginning of a new human being."[5]

HUMAN LIFE BEGINS AT FERTILIZATION

In surveying 5,577 biologists, researcher Steve Jacobs, a University of Chicago Ph.D., found that 96 percent of biologists affirmed that a human life begins at fertilization. Remarkably, the majority of the sample Jacobs polled identified as liberal (89 percent) and 85 percent identified as "pro-choice."[6] Not surprisingly, Jacobs came under fire in the media and from several of the outraged academics he had surveyed who apparently were "triggered" by the mere thought of being asked when a human life begins. But Jacobs' survey results only confirmed what human embryologists have known for decades: human life begins at conception.

However, despite the clear consensus of scientists, many people on both sides of the abortion debate remain confused about how and when human beings come to be. A popular youth speaker in the '70s and '80s was known for esteeming and encouraging those in his audiences by assuring them they were no accidents–they were here by divine appointment:

> "Do you realize you were once a sperm? That's right. You were once a sperm, and you were one of five million sperm all together in a group. Do you remember? All of you lined up at the starting line and at the end of a long, long tunnel, there was one egg. There was a race, and you won! Stop to think about that. The odds were five million to one and you came through. Your victory makes an Olympic gold medal look like nothing by comparison! You came through! You're a winner!"[7]

Although humorously entertaining, this common understanding of how we began is badly mistaken. According to the science of human embryology, you were never a sperm cell. This erroneous account of human development is a classic example of confusing parts with wholes. Like skin cells, sperm and egg cells are merely *parts* of human beings; they are not whole human beings. These cells or gametes, which combined or fused to create you, were functionally parts of other human beings, namely your parents. But when these cells came together and the process of fertilization was completed, conception occurred, and you came to be as a single-cell zygote. From this point forward, you had your own unique DNA. Your sex, race, and blood type were all determined–and each potentially different from your mother's. And although fully dependent upon your mother for blood, nutrients, oxygen, and the protection of her womb, you were unconsciously directing your own internal growth and development from the moment of conception on. Unlike the sperm or egg cells, you were a living organism–a whole human being–and not merely a part of something or someone else. American legal scholar and political philosopher, Robert George writes, "The difference between human gametes and a human being is a difference in kind, not a difference in stage of development. The difference between an embryonic human being (or a human fetus or infant) and an adult is merely a difference in stage of development."[8] In simpler terms, George is saying that sperm and egg cells are not human beings, whereas human embryos and human adults are equally whole human beings and differ only according to how developed they happen to be.

Maureen Condic, Assistant Professor of Neurobiology and Anatomy at the University of Utah, writes:

"From the earliest stages of development, human embryos clearly function as organisms. Embryos are not merely collections of human cells but living creatures with all the properties that define any organism as distinct from a group of cells; embryos are capable of growing, maturing, maintaining a physiologic balance between various organ systems, adapting to changing circumstances, and repairing injury. Mere groups of human cells do nothing like this under any circumstances."[9]

Therefore, the notion that you were once a sperm cell, or an egg cell is as scientifically inaccurate as claiming you were once your mother's kidney or your father's spleen. Scientific labels like zygote, blastocyst,[10] and fetus are strange to our ears. For this reason, these words, while legitimate and useful, can nonetheless have a dehumanizing effect on the tiny, developing human being. It is important to recognize that just like the words *infant*, *toddler*, and *senior citizen*, the words *zygote*, *blastocyst*, and *fetus* merely describe human beings like you and me at various earlier stages of our development.

YOU WERE NEVER A FERTILIZED EGG

Not only were you never an egg cell or a sperm cell, but you were also never a fertilized egg, even though this term is commonly used to refer to human beings at their earliest stage of development. A new human life begins at conception, which occurs sometime during fertilization. While human embryologists disagree on the precise moment within this 24-hour period that a new human being is conceived, until this occurs there is no human being, and after it occurs there is no longer a fertilized egg. At this point, the sperm and egg cells essentially die to themselves giving their constituents over to the creation of an entirely new entity or being, namely a tiny and immature but distinct, living, and genetically whole human being, called a zygote. Contrary to how many people view human development, our humanity does not come to us slowly or in part. Rather, it is who and what we are from our beginning. Robert George and Patrick Lee note: "A thing either is or is not a human being, that is, that each human being came to be at once, not gradually…A new human being does not 'partially' exist as the process unfolds. Rather, a new human being is what the process, if it reaches completion, brings into existence."[11]

So, we do not, as many imagine, start out as one kind of being, namely an alien-like "fertilized egg," and over nine months slowly gestate or morph into another kind of being, namely a human being. Instead, our lives begin at conception. Then, over the next nine months, and throughout our entire lives, we continue to develop and experience a myriad of changes. However, our nature and identity remain the same as the day we were conceived. As pro-life author and apologist Randy Alcorn states, "Something non-human doesn't become human by getting older and bigger. Whatever is human is human from the beginning."[12]

Therefore, to refer to the zygote or embryo as a "potential human being," as many do, is scientifically baseless. Although there was a time when you were a potential fifth grader, you were never a "potential human being" because, as celebrated geneticist Jérôme Lejeune points out: "There is . . . no pre-embryo, since by definition the embryo is the youngest form of a being."[13]

It is correct, then, to say that every human being from the point of conception is a unique, complete, one-of-a-kind human being, possessing a genetic blueprint that no other human (except in the case of cloning or monozygotic twins) has or will ever have. Therefore, Scott Klusendorf, president of Life Training Institute, is also correct when he states that, "Every 'successful' abortion ends the life of a living human being."[14]

LOOKS CAN BE DECEIVING

Some will still object and say the zygote, or early embryo, doesn't look like us. But this misses the point. What we look like at any stage of our development is irrelevant to what we are. Again, only objective, and scientifically measurable criteria can establish an accurate answer. For instance, just because some *thing* (say, a department store mannequin) looks like a human being doesn't mean that it is. Conversely, just because someone, such as a zygote, doesn't look like a human being, or how we think a human ought to look, doesn't mean that he or she is not a human being. Again, it was a failure on the part of his captors to understand this simple truth that cost Ota Benga his freedom. Science does not define or identify human beings or other species based solely on appearances. This is a good thing since we look very different at our various stages of development. Instead, science concerns itself with the actual nature or identity of the human being. And so, the question is not what does the zygote look like? The question is what is the zygote? To attempt to determine biological humanity based on one's size or physical appearance, as many abortion supporters do, would not be a scientific endeavor but a purely emotional or subjective one, which consistently and inevitably produces morally catastrophic results as history has repeatedly demonstrated.

But for the moment, let's set aside the consensus of human embryologists that human life begins at conception and that the zygote is a whole human being and return briefly to the bold claim no one knows when human life begins.

The inference of those who make such a claim is obvious enough: if people cannot agree on when human life begins, abortion must be morally permissible. Put another way, if something seems confusing, one is apparently free to do as one pleases. Again, even our Supreme Court applied this non sequitur in their *Roe v. Wade* decision. But wouldn't such a reckless conclusion nullify the need for justices and courts altogether? After all, if the judicial response to moral disagreement or confusion is unfettered moral autonomy for the plaintiff and defendant, what is left for the court to decide? Why don the black robes at all?

In truth, *Roe v. Wade* is hardly a position of moral neutrality as Blackmun believed. While claiming that the Justices were "not in a position to speculate as to the answer" of when human life begins that is precisely what they did. Although forbidding states from restricting abortion before the point of viability, *Roe* allowed states to restrict abortion after viability, as long as such restrictions do not prevent a woman from pursuing abortion to save her life or health. However, *Roe's* sister case, *Doe v. Bolton*, which was reached on the same day, defined "health" so broadly as to effectively prevent states from protecting fetal life at any stage of development. In other words, even if a state prohibits abortion in the third trimester, *Doe v. Bolton* made it legal for women to abort their children at this point since almost anything constitutes a health concern. Therefore, by permitting abortion for virtually any reason through all nine months of pregnancy, the Supreme Court did take a moral position on when human life begins. Practically speaking, they decided this magical moment occurs at birth, and not a minute sooner.

BLISSFUL IGNORANCE?

The seemingly harmless proclamation, "no one knows when human life begins," is a bold assertion that reveals a few things about those who make it.

To claim no one knows when human life begins is to number oneself among those who do not know. Therefore, this statement is valuable only to the extent that it serves as a personal confession. Just because the person making this claim doesn't know when life begins doesn't mean no one knows. Maybe somebody does know. I may not know how many bases Jackie Robinson stole during his major league career, but that doesn't mean no one knows. Or suppose someone asserts, "No one really knows if Mars is the fourth planet from the sun." The person who states this reveals only one thing: he doesn't know if Mars is the fourth planet from the sun. To assume no one else knows is at best ignorant and at worst arrogant. Astronomers, those most qualified to speak to the question of Mars' location in the solar system, declare that Mars is indeed the fourth planet from the sun. Consequentially, a responsible thinking person must necessarily assess the claims of such experts before rejecting (or for that matter, accepting) their claims about reality.

The consensus of embryologists, those within the scientific community most qualified to speak to this matter, is that human life begins at conception. Now it is possible the embryologists are wrong. But a rational person would require compelling reasons for rejecting their findings, especially when so much is at stake. Even prominent pro-abortion philosophers such as Peter Singer, professor of Bioethics at Princeton University, and David Boonin, professor of Philosophy at the University of Colorado Boulder, readily accept the consensus of human embryologists and acknowledge the full biological humanity of the zygote. Singer writes: "It is possible to give 'human being' a precise meaning . . . there is no doubt that from the first moments of its existence an embryo conceived from human sperm and eggs is a human being."[15] As an ardent defender of abortion, Singer is aware that such an admission does nothing to help his cause. However, he knows that he would jeopardize his credibility by denying the scientifically established fact that the embryo is a living human.

Finally, suppose we grant for the sake of argument the supposition that no one knows when life begins: Where does that leave us? Does it bolster the case for abortion? No. To the contrary, such a statement, if true, only serves as an argument against legalized abortion, not for it. Think about it. To argue "no one knows when life begins" is to concede the possibility human life does begin at conception. In other situations where we are not sure if there is human life, we always err on the side of life. Therefore, defending abortion with a proclamation that leaves open the possibility human life does begin at conception is like a hunter shooting into rustling bushes without first identifying the target. American philosopher Francis Beckwith illustrates this willful and reckless disregard for others by imagining a demolition team who'd be willing to detonate a building without first verifying no one is inside. Beckwith says it well: "If you're willing to engage in an act where you know there's at least a 50/50 chance of killing a human person that means you're willing to kill a human person."[16] Even the remote possibility that the zygote or embryo is a human being should restrain us from aborting until the question can be further investigated and answered with certainty. Ignorance is not bliss when human lives may be at stake. So, ironically, even if Justice Blackmun was correct that the question of when life begins is shrouded in mystery, this would only serve as a good reason to oppose abortion.

With that behind us, may we not forget that the scientific evidence for the full biological humanity of the zygote, the earliest developmental stage of a human being, is overwhelming. Nevertheless, while scientific evidence can establish when a human comes to be, it is incapable of establishing or determining human value. It is for this reason that Fr. Richard John Neuhaus states, "Establishing by clear evidence the moment at which a human life begins is not the end of the abortion debate. On the contrary, that is the point from which the debate begins."[17]

Neuhaus is right and for this reason we turn to chapter four to explore the foundation for human dignity and intrinsic moral worth.

CHAPTER 4
WHAT IF SUSAN COULDN'T SING?
THE CASE FOR HUMAN DIGNITY AND VALUE

O n April 11, 2009, an obscure, frumpy, middle-aged Scottish woman appeared as a contestant on the TV program, *Britain's Got Talent*. Susan Boyle marched nervously onto the stage before a panel of cynical judges and a live, mocking audience that afternoon. As she prepared to sing her rendition of "I Dreamed a Dream" from *Les Misérables*, the camera scanned the audience focusing briefly on one haughty young woman whose snickering face epitomized the contemptuous mood of many in attendance. Susan was in the lion's den.[1]

But then the music played and with the first golden syllable from her mouth, this ordinary woman astounded the audience, silencing those who had prejudged her. Indeed, Susan could sing. In that moment, Susan Boyle became a household name and an international sensation. Suddenly, the world loved her, or so it seemed. Afterward, shell-shocked judge, Piers Morgan, said, "Without a doubt that was the biggest surprise I have had in three years on this show. . . everyone was laughing at you. No one is laughing now."[2] Fellow judge, Simon Cowell, when rendering his vote of approval, patronizingly stated, "Susan Boyle, you can go back to the village with your head held high. It's three yeses!",[3] as if Susan's worth depended upon his and the other judges' validation. How arrogant of Simon, and how demeaning to Susan.

Interestingly, those who initially scorned Susan Boyle soon after congratulated themselves for their speedy character development. Days after her appearance, Piers Morgan confessed, "I think we owe her an apology because it was an amazing performance. As I said, we were all laughing at her when she started." Though Mr. Morgan strained out a gnat, he swallowed a camel.[4] The apology owed Susan was not for wrongly assuming she couldn't sing. It is for thinking she's only valuable because she can sing. But what if Susan couldn't sing? Would the mocking she endured have been justified?

WHAT GIVES US VALUE?

The cruel treatment Susan received raises a crucial question at the heart of the abortion debate: What makes humans valuable? Are we valuable because of what we can do–because we can sing, or because of some other distinction such as skin color or sex? Or are we valuable simply by virtue of being human?

In chapter three, we observed that embryologists consistently acknowledge the biological humanity of the zygote or early embryo. However, answering the moral question, "Is the zygote my neighbor?" requires us to first answer the question "What gives us value?" A deep line has been drawn in our cultural sand over how we value human beings and, particularly, how we value nascent human life. Is the offspring in the womb sacred? Is the unborn child, even at her earliest zygote stage of development, an intrinsically valuable person worthy of full moral respect? Or can she be experimented upon, destroyed, and discarded as medical waste?

With respect to determining the moral value of the unborn, people often make the same mistake the audience made in determining Susan's value: they confuse human value with human function. Instead of cherishing unborn human beings for what they are, most abortion supporters value them only for what they can do. In the context of the debate over abortion, these two diametrically opposed ways of viewing and valuing human beings are popularly referred to as the pro-life view and the pro-choice view. Christopher Kaczor, philosophy professor at Loyola Marymount University, aptly refers to these conflicting views as the "endowment" and "performance" accounts of human value, respectively.[5]

PERSONHOOD THEORY: A FALSE DICHOTOMY

Biologically speaking, we know what constitutes a human and when a human begins to exist. However, those who hold to the performance view draw a moral distinction[6] between humanness and personhood, arguing it is morally permissible to kill humans so long as they're not actual persons. Proponents of this position, a position referred to as *personhood theory*, insist that biology neither determines personhood nor warrants a right to life. According to this view, human worth is not intrinsic or "hard-wired," but is determined by one's usefulness or desirability to her mother—not all members of the species *homo sapiens* are persons deserving moral respect. The real-world consequence is that the only human beings granted this respect are those who pass certain subjective and arbitrary tests that the big and powerful establish for them. The unfit, those who do not measure up, are crushed like vermin, and disposed of like trash. The prejudicial malignancy of this view was subtly displayed by the judges and the audience on *Britain's Got Talent*, but it is thoroughly metastasized in elective abortion. The philosophical flaws in this view are many, but let's consider two of them.

First, advocates of the performance, or functionalist, approach do not offer sufficient reasons to accept their preferred test for inclusion in the human community as value-giving. For instance, Australian philosopher Peter Singer, writes, "Human babies are not born self-aware, or capable of grasping that they exist over time. They are not persons . . . The life of a newborn is of less value than the life of a pig, a dog, or a chimpanzee."[7] But why self-awareness? Why not something else, like viability or sentience? The best Singer has to offer by way of an answer is that beings (not limited to human beings) that are self-aware are valuable "persons" because they can experience pain and pleasure, because they prefer to live pleasurable lives, and because they prefer to stay alive. Singer further argued that newborns should not necessarily be considered persons until 28 days after birth. He writes,

> "When the death of a disabled infant will lead to the birth of another infant with better prospects of a happy life, the total amount of happiness will be higher if the disabled infant is killed. The loss of happy life for the first infant is outweighed by the gain of a happier life for the second. Therefore, if killing the hemophiliac infant has no adverse effect on others, it would, according to the total view, be right to kill him."[8]

For this reason, the late historian and syndicated columnist, Nat Hentoff, wittily referred to Singer as the "apostle of infanticide."[9] Of course, Singer's functionalist approach for determining personhood which he grounds in the fluctuating trait of self-awareness excludes many human beings, not just the unborn and newborns, from the community of rights-bearing persons while including some animals such as pigs, dogs, and chimpanzees.

Singer's approach is tantamount to judging a beauty pageant where each contestant's beauty is in the eye of the beholder. One judge prefers blondes, another prefers brunettes, but neither can provide persuasive scientific reasons or sound philosophical arguments for why their personal preference should crown the queen. This whimsical approach may be sufficient for picking a beauty queen, but it is hardly an objective or morally responsible method for determining who should live and who should die. It is difficult to escape the presumption of Peter Singer and others like him who claim to know with certitude which subjectively chosen "test" should rank human value. Regardless of the test or attribute posited, none seem compelling enough to create a consensus among abortion supporters. This lack of consensus is decidedly inconvenient for the unborn and exposes the fact that the only real test that matters is whether mom wants her baby to live. Nancy Pearcey, professor of apologetics at Houston Baptist University, sums up the problem: "The fact that bioethicists come to such wildly conflicting definitions of personhood shows that the concept is virtually impossible to define once it is cut off from the sheer fact of being biologically human."[10]

The second philosophical flaw is that the performance tests, such as Singer's appeal to self-awareness, are incapable of providing an unshakable foundation for human equality since they are nothing more than mutable measuring sticks for calculating human worth. Therefore, the pro-choice position is elitist and intolerant. These may be fighting words, but it is difficult to deny their veracity. For example, self-awareness does not come to every human being at the same time or to the same degree. Therefore, if self-awareness is what confers personhood status, then those who have more of it would have greater value and would be deserving of greater moral rights.[11] As a result, Kaczor points out that the performance approach not only divides us against one another, it divides us against ourselves.[12] Furthermore, self-awareness is not a permanent condition; it comes and goes depending upon one's circumstances.

AN ALL-OR-NOTHING PROPOSITION

Human equality is an all-or-nothing proposition. We cannot chip away at it, dissect it, or parse it out and, at the end of the day, have anything meaningful left of it. Every time society divides the room or the womb by subjective, fluctuating tests for inclusion in the human community–such as size, level of development, environment, or degree of dependency–the table legs are kicked out from under human equality and the weak and vulnerable are killed unjustly. Our world has a long history of defining entire classes of people out of existence simply because they do not pass someone's arbitrary test. Whenever humans are denied personhood status, innocent people die. The ovens of Auschwitz and the Atlantic slave trade bear witness to this fact. So do the dumpsters behind America's abortion clinics. Abortion supporters are often quick to express offense at such comparisons, but the parallels are inescapable.

Pearcey points out that when personhood theory determines human value, "Ultimately, someone will have to draw the line defining who qualifies as a person. But without objective criteria, the concept will be defined by raw power. Whoever has the most power– namely, the state–will decide who qualifies as a person."[13] If one's biology or humanness is insufficient for securing the right to life, then the state has become sovereign, and the individual has become expendable. Human rights are then reduced to mere privileges that the state sees fit to bestow, or revoke, at any given time. The primary role of government is to secure for its citizens the natural rights they have as human beings. A necessary result is that the laws and actions of government must protect the weak from the strong. But if being human is insufficient for securing the most fundamental right, then the role of the state is turned on its head. Now the state exists to protect the strong from the weak. This is the warped world of legalized abortion. Those who congratulate themselves for having moved beyond the bigotry of slavery now conveniently ignore or even defend the legal destruction of weak and vulnerable unborn children in the name of "choice" simply because they do not measure up to the subjective tests the strong and powerful have arbitrarily established for them.

In 1857, Supreme Court Justice Roger Taney argued that:

"[black people] were regarded as beings of an inferior order and altogether unfit to associate with the white race, either in social or political relations; and so far inferior, that they had no rights that the white man was bound to respect; and that the negro might justly and lawfully be reduced to slavery for his own benefit."[14]

Today we look with disdain upon such a shameful view of fellow human beings created in God's image. And yet, practically speaking, this is the same position the Supreme Court took in *Roe v. Wade* regarding unborn human beings. While pretending to be neutral on the question of when human life begins, they regarded the offspring of the womb as a being of an inferior order, unless of course her mother sees fit to bestow personhood status upon her. So inferior did our Court judge the embryo to be that she has no practical rights that even her own mother is bound to respect. Although slavery and racial segregation are embarrassing pockmarks on our nation's history, the same thinking that once put blacks into leg irons and onto the back of the bus now puts aborted children into incinerators and biohazard waste disposal bags. Like Justice Taney, who viewed the black man as property simply because of his skin color, those who defend abortion view unborn children with the same contempt simply because they do not function at their preferred level for inclusion in the human community. Or worse, because they view the unborn as an impediment to their own comfort or convenience. The targets of discrimination and oppression have changed but the bigotry remains the same.

Sadly, the audience's love for Susan Boyle was only skin deep. Like Ota, she had to perform to earn their accolades. She had to prove her value by entertaining them. This is precisely how our courts and much of our society treat unborn children. They are valuable only if we want them or if they serve some purpose toward the betterment of society.

But if we are going to insist on confusing one's value with one's function, why stop at abortion? What prevents us from applying this same thinking to those outside of the womb who can't sing or march to our drum? After all, this is the utilitarian position Singer and others like him are now advancing. As history teaches, ugly worldviews have ugly consequences, or more to the point, as Christian speaker and author John Stonestreet reminds us: "Ideas have consequences and bad ideas have victims."[15]

Standing opposed to the pro-choice position of functionalism or personhood theory is the pro-life position, which again, Kaczor fittingly refers to as the "endowment approach." This view teaches "beings with endowments that orient them towards moral values, such as rationality, autonomy, and respect, thereby merit inclusion as members of the moral community."[16] Being human is a sufficient, but not a necessary condition for being a person. In other words, while not every person is a human (angels are persons but are not human), every human is a person simply by virtue of being a member of the human community. Whereas the pro-choice view is subjectively and arbitrarily defined, the pro-life view is objectively grounded since being a human is an empirically discernable category–defined by the creation of a new individual human being at fertilization.

Our Founding Fathers recognized these God-given endowments and viewed them as the "self-evident" and unshakable foundation for human equality, motivating them to declare: "All men are created equal, and are endowed by their creator with certain unalienable rights"[17]–most notably the right to life. This view is non-discriminating and inclusive. Although those of us who subscribe to the endowment view of human persons are routinely portrayed in the media, in Hollywood films, and on university campuses as intolerant and hateful, the opposite is true. We are the tolerant ones. And, it is our view, not theirs, that provides the moral and philosophical framework for human equality. Again, the performance view puts innocent men, women, and children in leg irons; our view lets them out. Their view crushes precious children and exploits their young mothers during crises; our view loves, rescues, and cares for both (I expound on this in chapter six). In short, the pro-life position holds that every living human being, at every stage of development, and without qualification, has inherent moral worth and deserves legal protection.

HUMAN DOINGS OR HUMAN BEINGS?

My youngest daughter, Katerine, was born with cerebral palsy. As a result, she is unable to walk and has extremely limited use of her hands. Although an adult, Katerine functions mentally at the level of a four-year-old. Yet when my wife and I take Katerine to a restaurant or anywhere in public, perfect strangers frequently open doors for her. At concerts and sporting events she is sometimes ushered to the front to take the best seat in the house. Why such preferential treatment for a child bereft of any political power or celebrity status? It is because

God has placed in each of us a moral intuition that wells up when we see need, vulnerability, or disability. We naturally want to help. In fact, the greater the need, the greater our urge to help.

Unfortunately, not everyone responds to the voice of moral intuition. Katerine's biological father didn't. He abandoned her on the side of a road at 6:00 a.m. in Guatemala City, Guatemala, her birthplace, to fend for herself at six years of age. She was eventually discovered by a security guard and spent the entire day, until 10:00 p.m., in the police department before an orphanage was found that would take her. This is where she spent the next three years of her life. Katerine's father's actions are revolting, however, in many wombs she would have been aborted for the same reason her father abandoned her and for the same reason strangers now open doors for her: *she is less developed than most of us.* Simply because cerebral palsy severely arrested her level of development, Katerine would be considered by many to be disposable– "abortable"–as long as she was still in the womb.

But the pro-life position argues that Katerine's limitations neither alter her nature nor diminish her value. Katerine has inestimable worth simply because she is one of us. She is valuable, not because of what she can do, but simply because of what she is: God's image-bearer. We are not "human doings," we are human beings. This makes all the difference. As pro-life speaker and apologist Clinton Wilcox writes: "The question of when human life begins is not a difficult one to answer. It only becomes difficult if you want to justify killing people."[18] How true. My daughter escaped the womb with her cerebral palsy undetected. Many others aren't so lucky.

PICKING PHILOSOPHICALLY EMPTY POCKETS

Unfortunately, abortion supporters are not the only ones who confuse human value with human function; sometimes well-meaning pro-lifers do too. Consider the popular defense, articulated by the late pro-life columnist, Joseph Sobran:

"After tens of millions of [abortion] 'procedures,' has America lost anything? Another Edison perhaps? A Gershwin? A Babe Ruth? A Duke Ellington? As it is, we will never know what abortion has cost us all."[19]

In other words, abortion is bad because we might abort someone who might otherwise benefit us. Now to be fair, Sobran makes a good point: abortion has undoubtedly deprived us of countless intelligent and talented individuals who may have made our lives more fulfilling or exciting with new inventions and entertaining home runs. And as many pro-lifers point out, we may have aborted the person who would have developed a cure for cancer. All of this is bad to be sure. However, as Jay Watts, president of Merely Human Ministries, points out: "This is what's wrong with abortion, but this is not why abortion is wrong."[20] In other words, abortion is not wrong primarily because of what it costs *us*; it is wrong because of what it costs *those who are aborted*. While there are many things wrong with abortion (e.g., the possibility of aborting the next Einstein, the physical and emotional effects on post-abortive women and men, the economic impact on society, etc.), abortion is fundamentally wrong because it unjustly ends the life of an innocent human being. No qualifiers are needed.

Pro-lifers who employ this functionalist line of defense are guilty of picking the philosophically empty pockets of abortion supporters who argue that people matter only if they benefit others or society at large in some meaningful way. We do well to remember that this is their position, not ours. When human value is measured against the highly praised functional abilities of a Gershwin or a guy who entertains us by hitting homers, the unborn child loses–and yes, so does all of society. Whether those destroyed by abortion would have lived to become future inventors or future competitors in the Special Olympics is irrelevant. The pro-life position is tolerant and inclusive: Edison counts and so does the child with an extra chromosome.

Sobran meant well. But arguing as he did is not only philosophically weak, it is tactically risky since it invites our abortion-choice opponent to counterpunch with: "Sure, but abortion is a societal good because we might also abort the next Hitler. That would be a good thing, right?" Now we're at an impasse. When defending innocent human lives against abortion the best intentions aren't enough; we need the best arguments. These tiny womb dwellers are worthy of life and of our very best efforts, so let's not make the other side's job easier by pirating from their defective worldview to defend ours. Given the fact that so much rests on our ability to argue well on their behalf, we should advance our most persuasive arguments and avoid the bad ones. Granting the functionalist premises of our opponents will neither make our case nor refute theirs.

OUR VALUE CAME TO BE WHEN WE CAME TO BE

On May 24, 2009, Susan Boyle returned for a second visit to *Britain's Got Talent*. This time, her hair was styled, she was all made up, and she was wearing stylish clothes. The show's handlers had created her in the audience's image. The message to Susan and to women everywhere was loud and clear: your value is merely instrumental, not intrinsic.[21] Your worth is predicated on your looks and your ability to perform for us. With surgical skill, British journalist Tanya Gold took a scalpel to the hearts of many when she asked: "Is Susan Boyle ugly? Or are we?"[22]

In stark contrast, the pro-life position holds that Susan's value came to be when she came to be. Like the unborn, Susan has inherent moral worth and is equal both in nature and value to every other human being. Her worth is not dependent upon her physical beauty, gender, skin color, or her ability to sing. Susan Boyle, my daughter Katerine, and unborn children are beautiful and intrinsically valuable simply because they bear God's image. As a result, they deserve our love and protection. This is the pro-life message.

Jesus taught His disciples, "By this everyone will know that you are my disciples, if you love one another."[23] But we are not just to love one another; Jesus stretched the boundaries of our love to include outcasts, sinners, and even our persecutors. As Christians, we should apply our compassion consistently across the spectrum to all human beings as we recognize the worth of all humans as God's image bearers. And may the same hands that would open a door for a young girl in a wheelchair hold back the door of death as it slams on her no-less-human neighbors in the womb.

CHAPTER 5

MISSING PERSONS

WORDS AND IMAGES REVEAL ONLY A SLIVER OF
THE EVIL OF ABORTION

C hildren, especially newborns, have an almost magical ability to melt our hearts. Their sweet innocence and gentle features can tenderize even some of the crustiest people. Of course, there are exceptions. At times the very presence of babies, born and unborn, has hardened human hearts beyond comprehension, making monsters of men, or perhaps revealing the monsters they already were. For example, Pharaoh's lust for power caused him to order the Hebrew midwives to drown every newborn male in the Nile River, driving him even further into his own darkness.[1] Centuries later, the news of a newborn baby drove King Herod to madness, causing him to commission a killing squad to hunt down and slaughter every baby boy in Bethlehem under two years of age.[2]

Regrettably, cold-blooded child killers aren't confined to ancient history. Consider late-term abortionist and convicted murderer Kermit Gosnell. Gosnell is serving a life sentence in prison for delivering babies in his clinic and then murdering them by "snipping" (severing) their spinal cords with scissors. In their remarkable book, *Gosnell:*

The Untold Story of America's Most Prolific Serial Killer, authors Ann McElhinney and Phelim McAleer painstakingly recount the media-censored story of Gosnell's "house of horrors" abortion clinic in Philadelphia. Insulated for decades from any meaningful medical or legal accountability, Gosnell plied his grisly trade in his filth-ridden, flea-infested killing center where toilets were occasionally blocked with fetal remains and shelves were littered with his trophies; jars of formaldehyde containing the little feet of many of his victims. Although the name Kermit Gosnell is unknown to most Americans, his decades-long killing spree allegedly resulted in the murder of hundreds of innocent children in this manner, dwarfing the number of victims produced by serial killers Ted Bundy, Jeffery Dahmer, and John Wayne Gacy combined.

A MATTER OF GEOGRAPHY?

For obvious reasons, Planned Parenthood and their bedfellows in the media sought to distance themselves from Gosnell. In fact, some abortion supporters went so far as to try to pin the blame for Gosnell on pro-lifers. For example, author and lawyer Jill Filipovic, writing an opinion piece for *The Guardian* brazenly asserted that "widespread adoption of pro-life laws created . . . Gosnell." She also stated,

> "The braying about Gosnell is a ploy to shame the media into covering the issue from the anti-abortion perspective, conflating the illegal procedures performed by Gosnell with safe, legal abortion. That conflation is necessary for the pro-life side to use the media coverage to promote unnecessary regulations of clinics, purposed solely to make abortion less accessible, and advocate for the very things that allowed Gosnell's clinic to exist in the first place."[3]

Ms. Filipovic suffers from an acute case of denial. If anyone is guilty of conflating anything, it is she who conflates the legal butchery of innocent children with the guileful language of "safe, legal abortion." But no matter how one spins it, the cold fact is that murdering children in any location is an ugly business. Although attempting to normalize abortion by lumping it in with legitimate surgical procedures, Gosnell's own defense attorney, Jack McMahon, conceded this point. He argued that his client should not suffer legal consequences for "snipping" the spinal cords of children born alive in his clinic, and thereby killing them, since "Abortion—as is any surgical procedure—isn't pretty . . . It's bloody. It's real. But you have to transcend that."[4]

In an April 2013 USA Today article, political analyst Kirsten Powers, pointed out the moral schizophrenia of attempting to justify Gosnell's murder of children in one location while condemning it in another:

"Regardless of such quibbles about whether Gosnell was killing the infants one second after they left the womb instead of partially inside or completely inside the womb—as in a routine late-term abortion—is merely a matter of geography. That one is murder and the other is a legal procedure is morally irreconcilable."[5]

Powers is exactly right. Abortion is the only legal method of wantonly killing innocent human beings and bizarrely, its justification is based solely on the victim's location. In the United States a mother can lawfully have her son or daughter killed but only if he or she is in the womb, or at least in the birth canal. But emerging from the birth canal does nothing to change the human nature or intrinsic value of the one being killed, nor does being in the womb mitigate the injustice of such killing. Gosnell is guilty before our courts for brutally killing three infants on this side of the birth canal. He killed many others in this way according to the testimony of his staff, but the prosecution was only able to secure a conviction for the deaths of three of these little ones. However, Gosnell is guilty before Heaven's court for brutally murdering thousands of children on the other side of the birth canal as well. Contrary to what Ms. Filipovic asserts, Kermit Gosnell is not the anomaly or aberration she would have us believe him to be.

LOOSE LIPS SINK SHIPS

Consider circuit rider abortionist, Ulrich "George" Klopfer, who performed as many as 50,000 abortions over four decades, the majority of which were performed at his clinics in South Bend, Gary, and Fort Wayne, Indiana. In August 2016, Klopfer was called before the Indiana Medical Licensing Board for numerous reporting violations, including performing abortions on girls as young as 13 and not reporting them to the Department of Child Protective Services as required by law.

During this meeting, Klopfer admitted to not reporting child sexual abuse and to promoting ways to cover it up. His actions put these young girls at risk of being sent back into abusive, sexual relationships. Cathie Humbarger, who at that time served as the Executive Director of Allen County Right to Life, led the effort to expose Klopfer's illegal actions.

She attended this meeting and reported, "The board members were outraged, and rightly so. Klopfer's own words sealed his fate, and the board stripped him of his medical license."[6]

After his death in September 2019, authorities discovered 2,246 preserved aborted children in his home and an additional 165 in the trunk of his car.

The investigation found that these children were aborted by

Klopfer at his three Indiana clinics between 2000 and 2003. This means his tiny victims had been stored in his home and car for nearly two decades.

Repulsed by the satanic barbarism of men like Gosnell and Klopfer, we label them "bad seeds" and search frantically for some way to divorce them from our species. We're nothing like them, we assure ourselves. Or are we?

In the New Testament book of Romans, the apostle Paul writes of God's wrath being revealed from heaven against those who "suppress the truth by their wickedness." He describes these truth suppressors as full of "every kind of wickedness," full of "murder," and says, "they invent ways of doing evil."[7]

Since Cain attacked and killed his brother Abel, humans have become quite innovative in devising clever methods to kill each other.

And nowhere is this evil innovation more evident than in the sophisticated abortion techniques fallen mankind has devised to invade the womb and execute unborn children.

The medical terminology of vacuum aspiration, dilation & evacuation (D&E), dilation & extraction (D&X) conceal just a few of the demented methods invented to violently extract children from the womb.

WILLIE'S JESUS

Abortionist Willie Parker, in his book *Life's Work: A Moral Argument for Choice*, claims to be a Christian. He also claims Christ has called him to perform abortions, and likens himself to a "twenty-first-century Saint Paul, preaching the truth about reproductive rights."[8]

He writes warmly of "the Jesus I love," a Jesus who he argues "realizes that petty rules and laws laid down by the fathers and authorities are meaningless."[9]

Apparently, Parker's manufactured Jesus views the Sixth Commandment, "Thou shall not murder," as petty and meaningless. Parker has made Jesus in his own image—the epitome of idolatry.

Having freed himself from the commands of the real Jesus, who cherishes and protects children, Parker argues that an unborn child should be "imbued with sacredness only when the mother or the parents deem it so"[10]—a view that would justify killing any child of any age whose sacredness his or her mother does not acknowledge.

All the while Parker, a self-proclaimed "reproductive justice advocate," speaks eloquently of the "respect and compassion that should be accorded to every human being."

Like most abortion supporters, Parker loves his euphemisms, calling unborn children "products of conception" and innocuously referring to his twisting their heads and limbs off as "disarticulation." However, in his book he describes his abortion procedure with shocking candor:

> "I then open the cervix with a series of dilators . . . until the opening is as big as I need it to be, a measurement that correlates directly to the gestational age of the fetus . . . Then I insert a straw, called a cannula, through the opening and attach that to a suction tube, which leads to a canister by my feet. I flip a switch on the canister body, which turns on a vacuum, and, with a circular motion, I sweep the walls of the uterus with the tube. Within the space of a couple of minutes, the products of conception are sucked through the tube and into the canister."[11]

Parker continues by describing what he does after the abortion to prevent serious infection in the mother, a process he describes as being "as crucial as any other, because it assures me that I've done my job completely and well." He writes,

"I take the products of conception back to the lab . . . And there, I inspect what has just come out of the woman's body: what I'm looking for is the fetal sac, which, at a later gestational age, becomes the placenta, and, after nine weeks, every one of the fetal parts–head, body, limbs–like a puzzle that has to be put back together . . . I make sure I find every part, and I place them together, re-creating the fetus in the pan. I have done this so many times that it has become routine . . ."[12]

To speak of the ruthless dismemberment, decapitation, and disemboweling of precious unborn children as "routine" and to call it "reproductive justice" is barbaric. And to link such savagery to Christ is to court His wrath.

Former slave and celebrated abolitionist Frederick Douglass (1818-1895) wrote of the brutality visited upon slaves by their slaveholders 150 years ago.

He said slaveholders abused, raped, and even murdered them "with almost as much impunity as upon the deck of a pirate ship."[13]

There was no secret in 1860 about what was happening on plantations.

In fact, when slaves would escape, their slaveowners would brazenly run ads in the local newspapers offering rewards for their return and describing their missing slave as last seen wearing a neck collar and chains with scars on his back.

But, unlike the brutal treatment of slaves, the brutal treatment of the unborn by abortion remains well hidden from most Americans.

When it comes to the crime scene, abortion clinics have gotten smart about cleaning up exceedingly well after themselves.

As a result, most people never see what abortion does to children. This often profoundly cripples their concern for abortion's victims.

INEXPRESSIBLE EVIL

It seems today there is no appropriate time or place to show what abortion does to innocent children. The media, Hollywood, and our universities won't show abortion's victims. And to the delight of Planned Parenthood, most churches won't show them either. Interestingly, our eyes can gaze upon every other vile thing, no matter how graphic or disturbing. But apparently, we are too refined and too delicate to look at the ghastly effects of abortion. Even though victim imagery is effectively used to expose every other injustice, the majority of our churches and even a large swath of pro-life ministries have surrendered what is arguably our most powerful tool in changing hearts and minds on the evil injustice of abortion: the photographic evidence of the mangled bodies of aborted children. This is unfortunate to say the least, because as Gregg Cunningham, Executive Director of The Center for Bioethical Reform, says, "Everyone knows intuitively that abortion is evil. But almost no one knows how evil it is until they see it, because abortion is inexpressibly evil."[14]

A PICTURE PAINTS A THOUSAND INJUSTICES

Movie producers, educators, and social reformers the world over have used graphic victim imagery to expose injustice because they know what we all know instinctively: a picture paints a thousand words. *National Geographic's* striking 125th anniversary issue, entitled *The Photo Issue*, features a full-page quote from the widely acclaimed South African photographer Brent Stirton, which reads: "Photography is a weapon against what's wrong out there. It's a witness to bearing the truth."[15] His quote appears in relation to disturbing photos of a poached 500-pound gorilla in the Congo and a small herd of emaciated camels starving in Kuwait. Another full-page quote from award winning journalist and photographer Michael Nichols reads: "My pictures are about making people realize we've got to protect those who can't speak for themselves."[16] His quote appears next to a photo of an orphaned baby elephant whose mother was killed by poachers. Stirton and Nichols are right: photography is an indisputably "powerful weapon against what's wrong out there" to awaken us to "protect those who can't speak for themselves."

Unfortunately, this powerful weapon–so liberally employed to protect gorillas, camels, and baby elephants–is almost never employed to protect baby humans. Again, Gregg Cunningham points out, "When you hold up an aborted baby photo, abortion protests itself."[17] Abortion supporters understand this, which is why they work so aggressively to conceal these images. Surprisingly, however, feminist and abortion supporter Naomi Wolf readily concedes not only the power of abortion victim images, but the validity in using them to change hearts and minds:

> "The pro-choice movement often treats with contempt the pro-lifers' practice of holding up to our faces their disturbing graphics . . . How can we charge that it is vile and repulsive for pro-lifers to brandish vile and repulsive images if the images are real? To insist that the truth is in poor taste is the very height of hypocrisy. Besides, if these images are often the facts of the matter, and if we then claim that it is offensive for pro-choice women to be confronted by them, then we are making the judgment that women are too inherently weak to face a truth about which they have to make a grave decision."[18]

Wolf further states: "When someone holds up a model of a six-month-old fetus and a pair of surgical scissors, we say, 'choice,' and we lose."[19] Indeed, sunlight is the greatest disinfectant.

I frequently share a one-minute abortion victim-imagery video during my presentations. The video shows the victims of abortion in all three trimesters. It is difficult to watch. When introducing the video, I do three things. First, I make it clear that watching the video is optional. Those who prefer not to watch can simply avert their gaze or close their eyes. But I plead with those who have never seen abortion in all its ugliness to watch. Second, I contextualize why I am showing the victims; not to manipulate, but to educate. I point out what pro-life author Jonathan Van Maren, wisely states, "The history of social reform shows us that not a single injustice has ever been ended by covering up evidence of that injustice."[20] We could never begin to grasp the horrors of slavery, the Holocaust, or the terrorist attack on the World Trade Center and the Pentagon if it were not for graphic victim images. Some things are unpleasant to see but must be seen if we are to be moved from apathy to acts of love and compassion. Finally, I point those who have had abortions or have been responsible for abortion decisions to the forgiveness and healing Christ offers.

Each time I show my audiences the inexpressible evil of abortion, whether in a gymnasium packed full of students or in a conference room full of adults, the response is the same: stunned silence. This is because abortion is no longer abstract for those whose eyes have been opened. Showing abortion's victims provides the same service to my audiences that movies like *Schindler's List* and *The Passion of the Christ* provided to their audiences, the unvarnished truth. Audience members often thank me for introducing them to abortion's victims.

Once, after showing abortion's victims I was approached by a tall, muscular man who appeared to be in his early fifties. I had noticed him earlier as he appeared to be waiting around to talk with me. With remorse, he shared that he was responsible for seven abortions. Thankfully, however, his story didn't end there. Through tears of joy, this imposing figure of a man spoke warmly of the forgiveness and freedom he had found in Christ. I found myself feeling emotional too, for having been invited into this personal detail of his life. He thanked me for showing the video and expressed his hope that my having done so might prevent others from making the same decisions he now regretted.

If you have never seen what abortion does to unborn children, I encourage you to go to www.projectlifevoice.com and watch this powerful video titled, "This Is Abortion."

CADAVERS COMMUNICATE WHAT CAMERAS NEVER COULD

Many people, like me, change their mind about abortion when they see what it does to unborn children. But, that said, the strongest argument for using victim imagery to expose abortion is not a pragmatic one but a principled one; simply put, we are commanded to do so. Paul commands the Church in Ephesians 5:11 to "Have nothing to do with the fruitless deeds of darkness, but rather expose them." If the state-sanctioned murder of tiny children by abortion is not a fruitless deed of darkness, what is? If the Church will not expose this evil, who will?

For several years, I introduced the victims of abortion to my audiences by stating: "Nothing has the ability to awaken moral intuitions like an image." However, having made this statement countless times I eventually came to realize that it simply isn't true. Now to be clear, the use of victim imagery is indispensable in helping audiences see the injustice of abortion, and, in many cases, these images help those who have had abortions come to terms with the sin of abortion and their need for forgiveness. For these reasons, I continue to show images of abortion's victims whenever possible. But the fact is, there is one thing that can awaken moral intuitions over abortion even more powerfully than an image, and that is the bodies of the victims themselves.

A picture may paint a thousand words, but what photograph could ever capture the sweet fragrance of a flower or the rapturous melody of Handel's Messiah? As indispensable as both words and images are in exposing the injustice and bigotry of abortion, they could never tell the whole story. Not even ten thousand words or photos could adequately describe abortion. And, although we catch a glimpse of abortion's horror through the camera's lens, we remain comfortably protected from the stench of its noxious odor, from feeling the violent vibrations, and hearing the sucking sound of abortionist Willie Parker's suction machine "sweep the walls of the uterus."

Therefore, even when graphic abortion images are shown, the aborted unborn children are still missing from every pro-life protest or event. Their absence from the abortion debate provides a tremendous tactical advantage to abortion profiteers and their supporters who wrap the baby's dismembered body in sanitized euphemisms and argue that outlawing abortion will only drive women into "back alleys." This is precisely where they want abortion to stay–in the back alleys of our minds, safely quarantined from awakening our consciences. The fact that the mere images of abortion's victims are almost never shown in our churches or even at most pro-life events says something about how vile the real thing really is.

As mentioned in chapter one, my wife and I held an aborted child in our hands in 1992. The nameless little girl who we cradled in our hands had been aborted and discarded along with the day's trash. She was perfectly formed and lovely, except for the fact that she was dead and cold. Her body was limp and terribly discolored from the saline solution that burned her to death in her mother's womb. I've told this story many times. The raised eyebrows I occasionally encounter suggest some are more offended that somebody would lift a child from a dumpster than they are that somebody would put her there in the first place.

I wish I could bring this little one with me to my speaking engagements and hold her out for all to see. Again, the mere sequence of flat digitized images educates and evokes deep feelings about abortion. But imagine—please try to imagine—the impact of holding out the actual dismembered or burned body of a murdered child for all to gaze upon. Her lifeless presence would protest the evil done to her in a way no words or photographs ever could. After all, if a picture paints a thousand words, how many words might the corpse of an aborted child paint?

When abortion supporters speak of a "right to choose" they never feel compelled to finish the sentence. Of what *right* are they speaking? The so-called "right" to destroy a human being. This is the ultimate euphemism designed to stop the abortion conversation before it even starts. It is easy for smug politicians and elitist university professors to pontificate about a "woman's right to choose" when they never have to breathe in the repugnant smell of death or hold in their hands the mutilated victims of their treacherous worldview. So too, it is easy for pastors and Christians to stay silent and comfortably numb when they never have to feel the dead weight of an aborted child–perhaps from their own congregation–whose limbs dangle lifelessly from her torso. Regrettably, the one thing that might awaken the Church's conscience more effectively than an image of an aborted child is the very thing most Christians will certainly never encounter: the aborted child herself. Cadavers communicate what cameras never could.

THE GREATER INJUSTICE

Moreover, no number of pixels could help us see the greater crime of abortion, which is neither found in the violence of the act itself nor in the physical pain it inflicts, but in robbing another human being of the precious gift of life. This is so because the greater atrocity, or the greater injustice of abortion, is not found in the manner or method in which unborn children are killed, but in the fact that they are killed. Regardless of whatever futuristic innovative killing methods heartless men might devise, there will never be a morally right way to squeeze life from an unborn child. Abortion is not evil merely because of the gruesome nature of abortion techniques. Nor is it evil merely because of the physical pain it inflicts on innocent, unborn children. Abortion is evil simply because it intentionally and unjustly murders human beings.

When a child is killed by abortion, she loses everything. To rob a human being like the precious little girl in that back-alley dumpster in Detroit of her right to life is to rob and strip her of everything. It is to steal every human right, every joy, and every human experience from her: the opportunity to smell a flower, hit a baseball, ride a bike, graduate from school, pursue a career, get married, and the opportunity to one day produce children of her own. Abortion is an attack on humanity, but because these children bear God's image, abortion is ultimately an attack on God Himself. Abortion is the ultimate act of vandalism against our Creator. This is the greater transgression of abortion.

Abortion is evil. If the Church will not speak out boldly against it, we should not be surprised when words like "compassion" and "justice" have become synonyms for "murder" and "butchery," and when our children, in the name of Christ, treat our grandchildren worse than gorillas and believe they've acted virtuously for having done so.

CHAPTER 6

AMERICA'S FORCED ABORTION
POLICY

Wang Jun was an intelligent, soft-spoken businessman from China who I met on a flight to Los Angeles in 2016. After introducing ourselves, Wang Jun shared that he lived as an American citizen in Cincinnati and represented a large company in the United States with business interests in Shanghai where he spent much of his time. After I admitted my ignorance about life in China, he seemed pleased for the opportunity to educate me by kindly fielding my many questions.

Eventually, Wang Jun asked me a question; "What kind of work do you do?" I love this question and I have an answer that people on both sides of the political and moral aisle love; "I am in the human rights business, and I advocate for human equality." He gave an approving look. Next, I added that I advocate for the most marginalized and oppressed people group in our nation, the unborn. My answer seemed to stir some compulsion in Wang Jun to confess his nation's sins as he sheepishly mentioned China's notorious one-child policy. When I asked what he thought about the policy, rather than stating his moral position on it he instead revealed his embarrassment over it by eagerly announcing that it had recently been changed to a two-child policy. Next, in what appeared to be as much of an effort on his part to convince himself as to convince me, he stressed that the policy was needed for "population control." He assured me that the policy is only enforced among (a.k.a., forced upon) poorer families living in rural areas. In his thinking, targeting children for death who are gestating in the wombs of poverty-stricken women was apparently somehow less offensive. As we continued to talk, it became clear that Wang Jun's discomfort over his homeland's horrific population control efforts by forced abortion had nothing to do with the fact that babies were being killed, but only with the fact that mothers were not the ones making the decision to kill them.

The Communist Chinese leader, Deng Xiaoping, imposed the one-child policy in 1979 with the stated purpose of limiting family units to one child each. This is all too common of secular humanists; they are willing to destroy humans in their misguided effort to save humanity. Those who failed to comply with the policy by becoming pregnant with a second child faced severe fines, sterilization, and forced abortions. Xiaoping promoted and defended his policy by claiming it was needed to ensure that "the fruits of economic growth are not devoured by population growth"–typical doublespeak from a communist government that views the state as supreme and the individual as expendable. In other words, thanks to forced abortion, society is relieved of the excessive burden of having to share their food with the next generation.

The brutality of China's previous one-child policy is obvious enough. Even many abortion supporters found it highly objectionable. Revolting stories of Chinese women forcibly taken from their homes by so-called "family planning" officials only to have their babies forcibly and lethally removed from their wombs abound.

THE TRAGIC STORY OF FENG JIANMEI

For instance, in 2011 in Shanxi Province, China, Feng Jianmei became pregnant with her second child. Because she was in violation of China's strict one-child policy, Feng and her husband Deng Jiyuan, were ordered to pay a 40,000 yuan fine (nearly a year's wages for the average family in 2011) or have their baby aborted.

On June 2, 2012, unable to pay this enormous penalty, Feng, now seven months pregnant was visited at her home by officials who beat her, blindfolded her, and took her to an abortion clinic while her husband was away.

Upon her arrival, she was coerced to sign a medical agreement to have an abortion and was then forcibly held down while the abortionist injected an abortifacient drug into her womb, legally killing her baby. Soon after, Feng delivered her dead child.

A sickening photo of the despondent Feng Jianmei laying in her hospital bed with her aborted child lying lifelessly on a blood-soiled, plastic sheet beside her, powerfully exposed the cruel savagery of China's one-child policy.

Recognizing the public relations challenge Feng's story posed, Planned Parenthood suddenly became "woke" and felt compelled to distance themselves from China's forced-abortion practice by publishing the following statement:

"Planned Parenthood Federation of America opposes coercive and inhumane reproductive policies and practices, including China's one-child policy and the illegal practices of forced abortion and coerced birth control reported in some localities . . . The continued oppression of Chinese families through coercive reproductive policies must end."[1]

Their craftily scripted outrage is thin veneer. Remember, this is the same business that was caught red-handed ignoring reports of statutory rape, covering up sex-trafficking of minors, and selling fetal body parts. It is hard to imagine a more vicious enemy of children or a greater advocate of the violent use of force.

The graphic photo and Feng's tragic story eventually served to pressure China's Communist Party to liberalize the law in January 2016 to an only slightly less savage two-child policy. Then, on May 31, 2021, it was changed again to a three-child policy. While this is a positive development, Nancy Flanders of Live Action reminds us, "A three-child policy keeps the 'womb police' in business. They will still be tracking women's fertility and birth and punishing those who find themselves 'illegally pregnant."[2]

China's coercive and inhumane reproductive policies and practices (to borrow Planned Parenthood's wording) are inhumane, not only because of the horror they inflict on powerless and innocent mothers, but because of the horror they inflict on their powerless and innocent children. China's young mothers who have had their precious children violently ripped from their wombs have suffered an unspeakably grave injustice to be sure. It is difficult to imagine such terror. But what about the injustice done to their never-to-be-born babies? To take offense at China's forced abortion policy only because it violates the rights of mothers is to reduce the unborn child to a disposable, inanimate object. After all, if a woman is robbed of her purse, we rightly feel badly for her, but we feel nothing for her purse. Her purse is not the victim, she is. To find injustice only when a baby is killed without her mother's consent is to objectify and further demean abortion's primary victims.

Although he avoided saying so, Wang Jun was clearly and rightfully ashamed of his homeland's abortion laws, but not necessarily for all the right reasons. Abortion is evil whether a government forces it on pregnant mothers or whether a government sanctions a pregnant mother's decision to force it on the child she carries. In both cases, abortion is forced on a non-consenting child. That happens every time abortion happens.

CIVILIZED CHILD-KILLING?

Compared to China's one, two, or three-child policy, our abortion laws in the United States appear cultured or "civilized" to many Americans. After all, our government doesn't limit family size and women aren't pulled from their homes at gunpoint and forced by law to have abortions. Abortion is purely voluntary; it's all about "choice," we are told. Hence the popular abortion slogan, "My Body, My Choice!" which dehumanizes the unborn, deifies individual autonomy, and obliterates moral responsibility.

But in fact, America does have a forced-abortion policy. It's called *Roe v. Wade*. Together with its sister case, *Doe v. Bolton*, these notorious Supreme Court rulings effectively granted one class of our citizenry, namely mothers, the legal right to force death on another class of our citizenry, namely their unborn sons and daughters. Every abortion is a forced abortion since no child consents to being crushed, dismembered, and then pulled in pieces from his or her mother's womb.

In their effort to turn the tables, abortion supporters routinely accuse pro-lifers of forcing our religion or morality on others. This is an absurd claim. When we protest or share our opinion about abortion, we are not forcing anything on anyone. We are simply doing what everyone in this debate is doing, using our influence in the hope of persuading others. As Americans, we have as much right to use our best efforts to influence the public square as anyone else. This is the democratic process and at the end of the day no one is obligated–or forced–to agree with us. This noteworthy difference between persuasion and coercion is conveniently lost on many abortion supporters. When they protest or share their opinions, it is celebrated as freedom of speech; when we do it, we are accused of "forcing our religion on others."

Pro-lifers are also frequently castigated by our opponents as Neanderthals who want to "turn back the clock" and force impoverished women and those who have been raped and have conceived children into illegal and dangerous "back-alley" abortions. This is an outrageously unfair and intellectually disingenuous accusation for several reasons.

First, the claim that prohibiting abortion would force women into dangerous "back-alley" abortions demeans women. It assumes that women are either unwilling or incapable of obeying laws. This is absurd. Granted, there will always be lawbreakers among both sexes; however, if abortion is made illegal again it seems reasonable to assume that most women would remain law-abiding citizens just as they were prior to the legalization of abortion in 1973. As Greg Koukl, founder, and president of Stand to Reason, points out, "A woman is no more forced into the back alley when abortion is outlawed than a young man is forced to rob banks because the state won't put him on welfare. Both have other options."[3]

Second, it is the rapists–not pro-lifers–who force their wills on women, causing some to become pregnant. By also opposing abortion in this case, pro-lifers are not forcing their morality or religion on anyone. In fact, the opposite is true. We simply want to see innocent children protected from the illicit use of force. In short, we do not believe the violent and forceful act of rape against women justifies the violent and forceful act of abortion against unborn children.

Third, every death by abortion, legal or illegal, is a tragedy, which is precisely why pro-lifers oppose abortion. However, the emotionally charged claim that prior to *Roe* "five to ten thousand" women died each year from self-induced abortions with rusty coat hangers and botched "back-alley abortions" at the hands of "back-alley butchers" is an outrageous falsehood. Former abortionist, Dr. Bernard Nathanson, one of the leading architects of legalized abortion in America, is responsible for having fed this wildly inflated statistic to the sympathetic media in the late 1960's. After becoming pro-life, Nathanson admitted he and his colleagues intentionally fabricated the number of women who allegedly died because of illegal abortions. He stated, "I confess that I knew the figures were totally false, and I suppose that others did too if they stopped to think of it. But in the 'morality' of our revolution, it was a useful figure, widely accepted, so why go out of our way to correct it with honest statistics?"[4]

Even Mary Calderone, former director of Planned Parenthood, countered this falsehood in a July 1960 article in the American Journal of Public Health when she wrote,

> "Abortion is no longer a dangerous procedure. This applies not just to therapeutic abortions as performed in hospitals but also to so-called illegal abortions as done by physicians. In 1957 there were only 260 deaths in the whole country attributed to abortions of any kind."[5]

In fact, according to the Center for Disease Control and Prevention, 39 women died from illegal abortions in 1972, the year before *Roe v. Wade.*[6] These are hardly insignificant numbers, but they are a far cry from the 5,000 to 10,000 we so often hear about. Again, as mentioned in chapter four, those who argue that abortion should remain legal since women will get them anyway are in effect arguing that the role of government is to protect the strong as they forcefully attack and kill the weak. This is obscene.

Notice, too, the mainstream media never reports on young minor girls who are physically forced into abortion clinics by their parents, adult boyfriends, and pimps. Nor do they report the tragic stories of young girls sentenced to an ongoing cycle of rape and incest because their assailants force them to get abortions. And of course, the media is also curiously silent about abortionists who have forced abortions on women even after these women have changed their minds.

WHO'S FORCING WHO?

When it comes to legalized abortion, those who recognize the dignity of unborn babies and make efforts to defend them aren't exerting force; rather, it's the abortionist and those who deny the unborn their right to life who do so. *Roe v. Wade* was the result of nine men forcing their version of "morality" on millions of unborn children. Abortion is nothing less than the forcible violence of forceps crushing a child's skull, the forcible ripping of the tiny limbs from the victim's torso, and the unforgiving force of a suction aspiration vacuum sweeping the uterus clean of every sign of human life.

As if this is not bad enough, let me share three more examples where abortion supporters seek to force their "morality" on others.

First, physicians and medical personnel in the United States currently enjoy medical conscience rights that safeguard them from being forced to perform abortions or to assist in suicide. But if the abortion lobby has its way, the Hippocratic Oath and those who live by it will soon be sent packing. Many bioethicists and medical elites argue that personal morality has no place in medical practice. While accusing us of forcing our morality on others, they insist on forcing pro-life doctors, nurses, and pharmacists to choose between their principals and their professions. In their minds, there is no room for dissent or personal conviction.

And it is not just those in the medical profession whose livelihoods are threatened. Just ask the Little Sisters of the Poor. This humble order of Catholic nuns, devoted to serving the sick and elderly, spent almost a decade fending off legal attacks from the enemies of religious liberty. In 2013 the federal government came after the nuns because they refused to comply with a federal mandate in the Affordable Care Act (ACA) which forced employers to subsidize the provision of contraceptives, including abortifacient drugs, to their employees. Such a mandate violated Catholic Church teaching and the nuns' consciences. These peaceful nuns fought back and thankfully, after a long, grueling effort to save their ministry, the Supreme Court ruled in their favor 7-2 protecting their right to freely serve the elderly poor and dying without violating their consciences and without the imposing threat of having to pay exorbitant fines.

American lawyer and prolific author Wesley Smith points out, "Such a clarion witness is intolerable to those who want to weaponize medicine to impose secular individualistic and utilitarian values on all of society."[7] Clearly, when abortion supporters wax eloquent about a woman's "right to choose," the only "right" they are interested in securing is the state's right to exploit government power for their own selfish, ideological purposes and financial gain. This is accomplished by subjugating dissenting pro-life medical personnel, and others like the Little Sisters of the Poor, to deny their deepest moral convictions to participate in killing children.

Second, in recent years, legislators in Hawaii, Illinois, and California have passed laws to force pro-life pregnancy resource centers, and in some cases the churches that house these ministries, to advertise for abortion by requiring them to post signs notifying their clients how and where they can receive taxpayer-funded abortions. We can be thankful that pro-lifers fought back hard, arguing that these laws amount to nothing less than compelled speech. On June 25, 2018, in a

5-4 decision, the United States Supreme Court struck down these laws as a violation of the First Amendment. But these unrelenting attacks on free speech and religious liberty are further evidence that the abortion lobby wants to force pro-life pregnancy resource centers out of business.

Third, pro-abortion lawmakers continue to work tirelessly to force taxpayers to pay for abortions, thereby violating the moral convictions and religious beliefs of millions of Americans who oppose abortion. They do this despite the findings of a January 2018 Marist Poll stating 58 percent of Americans oppose using tax dollars for abortion.[8]

Yes, the United States has a forced-abortion policy. The abortion industry forces it's lethal will on helpless children. And this vile industry enjoys the support of a powerful abortion lobby that works tirelessly to force pro-life medical personnel to perform abortions and to force pro-life pregnancy resource centers to promote it. And this monstrous evil is protected by career politicians who want to force you to pay for it.

A FETUS FETISH?

Let me take this opportunity to respond to a related accusation. Not only are pro-lifers accused of wanting to deny women access to "safe and legal" abortions, but we are also accused of not caring about women and children after they have been born. The popularized version of this accusation says, "Pro-lifers aren't really pro-life; they're only pro birth."

Some lies are so outlandish and so demonstrably false that it's hard to imagine how anyone could believe them. This is a perfect example. We are often portrayed as unfeeling hypocrites afflicted with a "fetus fetish"–obsessed with saving the lives of the unborn while having no regard for children who have been born. Abortion supporters continue to spread this allegation with evangelistic fervor, causing untold damage to the pro-life movement. In fact, it is repeated so often and by so many that its truthfulness is seldom questioned even among Christians. But as one author noted, "This criticism is about as flawed as it is popular."[9] A closer look reveals three flaws behind this harmful deception.

First, even if true, this does nothing to reform or sanctify the evil act of abortion. Suppose all pro-lifers were hypocrites and really didn't care about babies after they're born. How would this justify abortion? How could the corrupt character of pro-lifers justify the corrupt actions of the abortionist? It simply doesn't follow that one's supposed disregard for babies after they are born somehow justifies another's legal destruction of babies before they are born.

Second, this charge is a disingenuous effort to distract and to destroy our life-saving influence. Those who advance this argument say things like, "You're not really pro-life unless you also oppose war, the death penalty, and gun rights; and unless you support open borders, universal healthcare, and adopt every unwanted child." As pro-life speaker and author, Dr. Marc Newman, explains, their list goes on and on, taking us down "a slippery, never-ending, qualifier-laden slope".[10] It is important to understand what is at play here. This is an attempt on the part of our critics to redefine for us what they think it should mean to be pro-life, and to do so in such a way as to gut our effectiveness.

Pro-life apologist Francis Beckwith calls this "the fallacy of pro-life exceptionalism,"[11] namely that pro-lifers must address every moral wrong along with abortion to be morally authentic, but those who address any other moral wrong except abortion don't have to address abortion to be morally authentic. No other movement is held to this unreasonable standard. This criticism only seems to travel in one direction as those advancing this argument would never dare lecture those campaigning against homelessness, by arguing, "You don't really care about homeless people unless you also oppose abortion with equal fervor." No, you'll never hear this because only the unborn are treated with such scorn. Randy Alcorn, offers a great response, "To be pro-life should certainly mean more than being concerned for unborn babies, but it should never mean less."[12]

Third, pro-lifers lead the way in caring for mothers and for babies, both born and unborn. Former Michigan governor and political commentator, Jennifer Granholm, says she is "troubled and perplexed" over the distinction pro-lifers draw between "vulnerable children outside of the womb" and "those not yet born," a distinction she says is "represented by the cervical wall." She argues that pro-lifers only care about children inside "the cervical wall" while ignoring the needs of those outside of it. She asserts that the "obsession with being pro-life lasts about nine months, and after that it's each baby for herself . . . Shouldn't those who are concerned about the lives of the unborn be equally concerned about the lives of the recently born?"[13] This narrative may play well in the media and in women's studies programs on university campuses, but it doesn't pass the smell test. Jennifer wants her audience to believe pro-lifers are hypocrites, but let's follow the money to see who the real friend of women and children on both sides of the cervical wall is.

FOLLOW THE MONEY

Today there are approximately 700 abortion clinics[14] in the United States. Many of these are owned by men who profit handsomely from young women in crisis and from the blood of their children. Abortion is an incredibly lucrative business and as a result many of these abortionists drive expensive sports cars and reside in gated communities.

Conversely, there are approximately 2,200 pregnancy help organizations in the United States, many having more than one location, bringing the total number of pregnancy help centers to 2,800, four times the number of abortion clinics. Most of these ministries are led by women, for women, at no cost to women. There are no cash registers in these centers because all their services, including pregnancy testing, counseling, ultrasounds, parenting classes, diapers, clothing, etc., are free. Moreover, most of these centers are led by modestly paid staff members whose ranks are filled with volunteers of all stripes. Can there be any doubt about what motivates these selfless servants?

The Pregnancy Support Center of Lebanon, Missouri, is just one example of the sacrificial love the pro-life movement shows to young mothers and to their children. In addition to providing each of the services listed in the previous paragraph, they have also established My Sister's House, –a maternity home for pregnant mothers, and Project Thrive, –a housing program with 6 apartments for single moms and their children. These vital programs help women develop important life skills, pursue college degrees, and find fulfilling and meaningful employment, with the goal of providing a brighter future for them and for their babies. This ministry is remarkable, but it is not alone; many pregnancy centers have ministries like this. Additionally, there are approximately 400 maternity homes in the United States. And we need not waste our breath asking why Planned Parenthood's services are so expensive, or why they don't establish maternity homes: both the money trail and the blood trail lead directly to their door.

When it comes to caring for children, born and unborn, the real hypocrisy is not found among pro-lifers, but among abortion supporters who have the audacity to lecture us about authenticity while defending treating the unborn with all the tenderness of a pack of wolves, while doing virtually nothing to better the lives of the already born. And again, as if this were not bad enough, the abortion lobby continues their crusade to force (there's that word again!) out of business the very pregnancy centers that do the work they refuse to do.

In response to those outside and inside the Church who complain that pro-lifers focus too narrowly on saving the unborn, we should simply point out what should be obvious; we focus our energies and resources narrowly on rescuing the unborn because the abortion industry focuses their energies and resources narrowly on killing them.

Finally, despite the relentless efforts of abortion supporters to malign our character and undermine our ministry effectiveness, we devote our time and resources to helping young mothers and their children, born and unborn. Unlike the abortion industry, the pro-life movement is not motivated by greed or money. Nor are we motivated by the perceived "benefit" abortion affords women and men who want to behave as they wish sexually while emancipating themselves from the responsibility of caring for the children they create.

As pro-lifers we don't want to force our wills on anyone. We simply want to ensure that the small and vulnerable are protected from the crushing, lethal force of abortion by the big and powerful.

CHAPTER 7

"MY NAME IS IDIOT"

THE DEHUMANIZING EFFECTS OF LEGALIZED ABORTION - PART 1

O n August 18, 2016, news outlets reported a sickening story about a 4-year-old Arkansas girl taken into protective custody after having been zip-tied to her bed as a punishment by her mother and the mother's boyfriend. The malnourished child was found with deep purple bruising on her bottom, lower back, and legs. She also had a black eye, swollen cheek, bruised forehead, scars on her back, and dried blood on her lips.

As deplorable as this story is, however, it is hardly newsworthy in a society where child-abuse cases are all too common. But what elevated this story to a national news item is the fact that when police officers asked for this little one's name, she answered that her name was "Idiot." Upon further investigation, it was discovered that the mother's boyfriend referred to her daughter as "Idiot" so often she thought this was her name. It's difficult to imagine a story that could more forcefully demonstrate the dark capacity of the sinful human heart and the dystopian society it is producing.

WHAT'S IN A NAME?

Throughout history, the relentless effort to dehumanize humans by redefining them has spawned numerous and unspeakable atrocities. In Germany, the Nazis labeled the Jews "rats" and "useless eaters." Rwanda's Tutsis were called "cockroaches." In our own land, black people were dehumanized as "chattel." Joseph Fletcher, the radical father of the modern bioethics movement also found the "idiot" label useful for his purposes when he referred to the profoundly mentally disabled in this way and brazenly declared them to be "not human."[1] Dehumanizing words like these helped pave the way for slavery, rape, and massive genocidal campaigns. The rhetorical question, "What's in a name?" assumes the answer, "Not much." But when the name obliterates respect for intrinsic human value, setting the stage for child-abuse and murder, the answer is, "Everything!" And whether the denigrating name is spoken by mothers and their evil boyfriends, or by evil dictators, scientists, politicians, or abortion supporters, the consequences are devastating.

In a culture like ours where abortion is legal and common there is a sense in which no one escapes the dehumanizing effects of abortion. The abortionist's menacing fingers, and torturous tools of death reach far beyond the womb and into our university classrooms, our nation's highest court, and even our churches, leaving virtually no one untouched. This is so because the legal destruction of the weak and vulnerable by abortion is the predictable and inevitable outcome of a materialistic worldview that downgrades human beings to the mere products of impersonal evolutionary forces. We often hear from proponents of abortion that the human embryo is "just a collection of cells." No immaterial soul, no objective value, just protoplasm. This depressing view of human nature–which is the logical conclusion of materialism–strips each of us of our dignity as God's image-bearers. The result is that the weak and vulnerable among us become expendable–even disposable–at the hands of whoever holds the power.

ABORTION DEHUMANIZES CHILDREN

Consider the name-calling of abortion supporters here in the United States, who for decades have downgraded unborn children with cunning words like, "blob of tissue," "product of conception," and "parasite." In recent years, these euphemisms have been added to with a fresh batch of sanitized labels such as "uterine contents" and "medical waste." This has contributed to the deaths of over 61 million dead children and counting. But this dehumanization is not limited to children in the womb. Legalized abortion has a dehumanizing impact on children outside of the womb, too.

We are frequently told that we need abortion because legalized abortion reduces the number of unwanted children, thereby limiting the number of children who might suffer from child-abuse or neglect. In 1973, Larry Lader, co-founder of NARAL Pro-Choice America, assured Americans that the "abortion revolution" would usher in a utopia for children:

> "The impact of the abortion revolution may be to too vast to assess immediately. It should usher in an era when every child will be wanted, loved, and properly cared for; when the incidence of infanticides and battered children should be sharply reduced."[2]

America's sewers and abortion clinic dumpsters tell a radically different story. The irony in claiming abortion prevents child-abuse could not be more obvious since abortion itself is the ultimate child-abuse. But leaving this important fact aside, legalized abortion has had a devastating impact on children outside of the womb as well. Child-abuse cases like the deplorable story from Arkansas have continued to skyrocket since the 1973 *Roe v. Wade* decision. Since then, the number of reported cases of child-abuse and neglect has risen from 167,000 cases annually to nearly 700,000. According to the Children's Defense Fund, "a child is abused or neglected every 47 seconds in America—1,844 each day. In 2018, more than 673,000 children became victims of abuse or neglect . . . Infants were disproportionately victimized, with 15.3 percent of cases involving children under 1."[3]

Abortion supporters often respond to this dramatic increase in violence against born children by arguing that correlation doesn't equal causation; that many factors contribute to the rise in reported child-abuse cases. This is undoubtedly true. But regardless of how these statistics are interpreted, what is clear is that legalizing abortion has not had the expected outcome of reducing cases of child-abuse, since the number of child-abuse cases has risen dramatically since 1973. Furthermore, there is a compelling reason to connect the two. After all, what would cause us to believe a society that legalizes abusing children to death in one location (in the womb) would somehow cherish them and refrain from abusing them in another location (out of the womb)?

Our society's expressed moral outrage over a 4-year-old being called "Idiot" and physically abused might be convincing if not for the fact that four years earlier this same child could have been labeled "medical waste" and been legally abused to death in her mother's womb, and with no attention from our nation's news outlets. After all, the moral distance between calling a 4-year-old an "idiot" and zip-tying her to the bed is no farther than the moral distance between referring to unborn children as "medical waste" and dismembering them in their mother's wombs. Abortion is the great dehumanizer indeed, and innocent unborn children–many from our own churches– are abortion's primary victims.

ABORTION DEHUMANIZES WOMEN

But it is not just children whom abortion dehumanizes. It also dehumanizes women. Consider how abortion-on-demand has served to further objectify women by enabling soulless men to use and abuse them and then refuse to take on adult responsibilities. For example, in his online article, "6 Reasons Why We Should Support Abortion," Edward Thatch (presumably a pseudonym) connects the vile mentality of debased men like himself who view women as mere objects for sexual gratification with enthusiastic support for abortion. Disgustingly, he writes, "Abortion saves men from having to transfer wealth to sluts," and, "most abortions are saving a lot of alpha players from having to write a check to a single mom who is already getting a check from some other poor schlep."[4] Of course, it is no surprise that wicked men who see women as nothing but repositories for their animal passions would also view the children they create with as much disdain.

In addition, abortion dehumanizes women by displacing their God-given maternal instinct and transforming the womb into a bloody battlefield, pitting mothers against their own offspring. For decades, legalized abortion has been slickly marketed or packaged by the radi-calized feminist movement and the abortion industry as empowerment for women and freedom from the oppressive patriarchy. Ironically, the very movement that claims to champion equality for women views women as inherently incomplete. Equality and fulfillment, abortion supporters argue, can only be realized by granting mothers the legal right to impose lethal force against their offspring. The International Planned Parenthood Federation states on their website, "Denying women the ability to choose to end an unwanted pregnancy under safe and legal conditions is a violation of human rights and flies in the face of the empowerment agenda."[5]

Lila Rose, president of Live Action, confronts the notion that women need a little something extra–namely abortion–to measure up to men:

> "The biological reality of our bodies is not a threat to our freedom. The idea that women need the same 'ability' as men to not carry a child for nine months is absurd. On the contrary—that women can carry children is an ability, an amazing gift. It is not something to be mocked, controverted, and disabled."[6]

Lila couldn't be more correct. Jeffrey Ventrella, from Alliance Defending Freedom, adds, "When the most dangerous place for a young person today is in his mother's womb, that is a work of the devil."[7] So true. When it comes to abortion empowering women, the devil is in the details, as evidenced in a heartbreaking story told to me by a woman who approached me after I spoke at a church in Michigan. I share her story with her permission, though I've changed her name.

Laura's childhood innocence was stolen by a string of her mother's boyfriends who repeatedly molested and raped her. Her own mother turned a blind eye to Laura's abuse, and in 1977, at only 12 years of age, Laura became pregnant. Realizing the legal consequences and the relational upheaval this could cause, five months into Laura's pregnancy her mother put her in the car and drove her to

Planned Parenthood. Laura had no idea where she was going or what was about to transpire, but she remembers having to sign something at that clinic at the tender age of twelve. Before long, this little girl who should have been home playing with neighborhood friends was instead lying on a surgical table experiencing tremendous physical and emotional pain while her mother sat next to the abortionist and coldly narrated the horrific details of her abortion to her.

Nothing could be added to this story to make it any worse, except for the pitiful fact that this scenario was repeated two more times during Laura's childhood: two more times she became pregnant by her mother's perverted boyfriends and underwent forced abortions! As Laura pointed out to me, had abortion been illegal the abuse would likely have ended, her abuser would have been locked up, and her first child would be alive today. Instead, the only "empowerment" realized was by the men who raped her and by the abortionists who killed her children for financial profit.

Thankfully, the night before Laura's 14th birthday a friend encouraged her to put her trust in Christ. On that night, the One who promises to give rest to those who are weary and burdened[8] began His sanctifying work in Laura. As a result, she has experienced His comfort and healing and is now happily married to a godly man. Laura's story is living proof that abortion does not empower women or little girls; it makes them victims. For all its bluster, many of Big Abortion's victims are those it claims to champion.

Biased studies led by those who benefit financially or in other ways from abortion are often touted as conclusive evidence that abortion has little, if any, long-term physical, emotional or psychological impact on women. For instance, the often-praised Turnaway Study[9] led by researcher and pro-abortion activist, Diana Greene Foster, PhD, boldly claims that 95% of women who had abortions did not regret them five years later. Planned Parenthood claims on their website, "In-clinic abortion is a very safe, simple, and common procedure. . ." and, "Unless there's a rare and serious complication that's not treated, there's no risk to your future pregnancies or to your overall health."[10]

Despite these audacious claims, many women do regret their abortions. The medical and sociological evidence as well as the real-life experiences of countless post-abortive women prove that abortion harms women physically, psychologically, spiritually, and relationally. I have spoken with countless women over the past decade and have heard their personal stories of heartache and regret.

A 2011 study published in the British Journal of Psychiatry found that "women who had undergone an abortion experienced an 81 percent increased risk of mental health problems, and nearly 10 percent of the incidence of mental health problems was shown to be directly attributable to abortion."[11]

Other studies indicate post-abortive women are at a much higher risk of suicide. For example, a study published in the British Medical Journal in 2013 found "The suicide rate after an abortion was three times the general suicide rate and six times that associated with birth."[12]

Furthermore, many women have been severely physically injured and have even died from complications related to so-called "safe and legal" abortion. Karnamaya Mongar 41, an immigrant from Bhutan survived war in her native country only to die at the hands of abortionist Kermit Gosnell in 2009 after suffering cardiac arrest during her abortion procedure, according to the woman who administered her medication that day.

In 2013, Jennifer Morbelli, 29, died from a 33-week late-term abortion by abortionist Leroy Carhart. In 2017, 23-year-old Keisha Atkins died after an elective late-term abortion. According to the U.S.

Food and Drug Administration, at least 24 women had died from the abortion pill, Mifeprex, by 2018.[13]

Those in the abortion industry want to bury these stories along with the bodies of their victims, but, much to the chagrin of Big Abortion, facts, unlike people, cannot be killed.

ABORTION DEHUMANIZES MEN

Abortion dehumanizes men, too. First, *Roe v. Wade* has fundamentally stripped good and responsible fathers of their legal right to protect and provide for the children they helped create. I have witnessed young fathers outside abortion clinics who wept and pleaded with their wives and girlfriends for the lives of their unborn children, but in most cases to no avail. A man in his 50's once shared with me that when he was a young man, he had gotten his girlfriend pregnant. Despite pleading for his child's life, she made the decision to abort their child. Lamenting the painful loss of his child over 30 years later, he said to me with great emotion, "Before long I will be extinct and there will be no one like me left on the earth to carry on my name." This painful cry of the heart revealed the helplessness a father feels when the law prevents him from being able to protect his own child from abortion.

In a world that cries foul at even the least injustice (or perceived injustice) with respect to equality between the sexes, men are clearly not equal before the law when it comes to protecting their children. They are in fact denied every legal right as the fathers of their unborn children, unless of course, the mother chooses not to abort their child. In this case, the father is legally obligated to provide financially for his child for the next 18 years. To be clear, men should be responsible in this way and deadbeat dads should be prosecuted. But this lawful disenfranchisement–stripping men of their fundamental right and moral duty to protect their children–is a social castration of manhood and a scourge on the family.

A second way abortion dehumanizes men is by attacking male leadership in the home and in society by transforming many men into "moral Houdini's"–escape artists. It provides cover for those who prefer to use women to satisfy their carnal lusts and then squirm and wiggle out of their most solemn duty: to provide for and to protect the children they helped create. Practically speaking, the woman's so-called "right to abortion" becomes the man's "right" to perpetual childhood, or worse. As was the case with Laura's assailants, legal-ized abortion provided cover for immoral men to continue to inflict, with impunity, more abuse and death on her and her unborn children.

ABORTION DEHUMANIZES THE ABORTIONIST

And of course, in his dehumanizing treatment of the children he kills, the abortionist dehumanizes himself. In his booklet, *Thoughts Upon the African Slave Trade*, John Newton, former slave-trader and author of the beloved Christian hymn, "Amazing Grace," describes the self-inflicted, soul-eating effects of brutalizing other human beings for personal gain:

> "I know of no method of getting money, not even that of robbing for
> it upon the highway, which has so direct a tendency to efface the
> moral sense, to rob the heart of every gentle and humane
> disposition, and to harden it, like steel, against all impressions of
> sensibility."[14]

To tear children limb from limb from their mothers' wombs is to "efface the moral sense" and to "rob the heart of every gentle and humane disposition."

Notorious late-term abortionist Warren Hern is a case-in-point. Apparently robbed of every gentle and humane disposition, he readily concedes that abortion is an act of destruction yet complains that some of his colleagues in the medical field have "strong personal reservations" about inflicting this act of violence on tiny humans, whom he describes as having a "form . . . similar to our own." He writes,

> "We have produced an unusual dilemma. A procedure is rapidly becoming recognized as the procedure of choice in late abortion, but those capable of performing or assisting with the procedure are having strong personal reservations about participating in an operation which they view as destructive and violent . . . Some part of our cultural and perhaps even biological heritage recoils at a destructive operation on a form that is similar to our own . . . No one who has not performed this procedure can know what it is like or what it means . . . We have reached a point in this particular technology where there is no possibility of denial of an act of destruction by the operator. It is before one's eyes. The sensations of dismemberment flow through the forceps like electric current . . ."[15]

Unfortunately, the "sensations of dismemberment" that flow through Warren Hern's forceps "like an electric current" as he brutalizes his victims have not been powerful enough to awaken his own conscience. His moral nerve endings have been hardened "like steel, against all impressions of sensibility." This is the inescapable effect of abortion on the abortionist.

Another case-in-point is Planned Parenthood abortionist and Senior Director of Medical Services, Debra Nucatola. In a 2015 sting video produced by David Daleiden, President of The Center for Medical Progress, Nucatola is caught cavalierly discussing how she harvests the body parts of the children she aborts to further line her pockets. In the words of Eliza Martinez, Executive Director, New Mexico Alliance for Life, Nucatola is seen "swilling a glass of wine and munching on salad" as she heartlessly boasts, "We've been very good at getting heart, lung, liver, because we know that, so I'm not gonna crush that part, I'm gonna basically crush below, I'm gonna crush above, and I'm gonna see if I can get it all intact."[16]

Numerous other disturbing instances of the soul-eating effects of abortion on the abortionists themselves could be given. But you get the point; the abortionist does not merely ravage his tiny victims; he inevitably and unwittingly ravages his own soul in the process. To quote Frederick Douglass, "No man can put a chain about the ankle of his fellow man without at last finding the other end fastened about his own neck."[17]

WORDS MATTER

The Christian worldview protests this madness. It contends that all lives matter: black or white, rich or poor, Jew or Gentile, born or unborn. It further contends that words matter. Just as demeaning words have serious implications, so do accurate ones. To acknowledge the humanity of unborn children is to call them our neighbors. According to Jesus, this requires something of us: faithful Christians are to love their neighbors as themselves, whether that neighbor has been beaten and abandoned in a ditch or relabeled and abandoned in the womb. Both the love of Christ and a love for Christ require us to see the unborn through His eyes—not as an inconvenience or an embarrassment, but as precious brothers and sisters worthy of our love and protection.

Finally, because the 4-year-old girl from Arkansas was a minor, news outlets did not publish her name, but you can be sure that it is not "Idiot." God knows her name and she is precious to Him. Hopefully, someday this wounded little one will come to know Christ and the solace He provides. Then she'll sing with the hymn writer, "My name is graven on His hands, my name is written on His heart. I know that while in Heaven He stands no tongue can bid me thence depart."[18]

CHAPTER 8
THE ONES WE'RE ASHAMED OF
THE DEHUMANIZING EFFECTS OF LEGALIZED ABORTION - PART 2

It is not just the unborn, their mothers and fathers, and the abortionist who are dehumanized by abortion. Christians who remain indifferent are dehumanized as well.

In the summer of 1967 Bobby Gentry's song, "Ode to Billy Joe," soared to the top of the charts and became an international hit, pushing the Beatles' "All You Need is Love" out of its number one spot on the pop charts. My dad bought the vinyl record and played it religiously for weeks. The haunting melody and shadowy storyline captivated me as a young boy. Sung in first person narrative, a teenage girl tells the story of her family sitting at the dinner table as "Mama" breaks the tragic news that a neighboring teenage boy, "Billy Joe McAllister, jumped off the Tallahatchie Bridge" to his untimely death. This shocking news is contrasted against the banality of mundane life and casual suppertime conversation. No one seems very moved by Billy Joe's death. The brother responds indifferently by asking for "another piece-a apple pie" and all "Papa" can say is, "Well, Billy Joe never had a lick of sense, pass the biscuits, please".

It's a catchy but disturbing song that no longer enjoys much airplay, but this fictional family's ho-hum response to the heart-breaking news of Billy Joe McAllister's suicide reflects the attitude many Christians have toward the unborn. On the list of moral or social injustices, abortion ranks at the very bottom in many churches, if it ranks at all. Greg Koukl rightly describes abortion as a "yawner" for most Christians. He writes, "Mention the word 'abortion' . . . and eyes glaze over."[1] He's right.

When it comes to speaking up for the "least of these" of whom Christ spoke so tenderly–and with such a protective voice–many shepherds have become tongue-tied. As a result, many in their congregations have followed suit. It is no secret that the vast majority of Catholic, Protestant, and Evangelical churches, universities, and seminaries remain indifferent over abortion. Although many of them have impressive pro-life positional statements in their constitutions or catechisms, few do anything to stop the killing even within their own four walls.

OUR WICKED WORLD

Most of us have visited birthing centers at hospitals to welcome and celebrate new arrivals to our own families or to those of our friends. Upon arriving, we are often greeted by locked doors. Before being allowed entrance, we must push a button, identify ourselves, and wait to be "buzzed" in by security or nursing staff. When we're ready to leave, the procedure is repeated, but in reverse; we must push the button and be "buzzed" out. This is not unusual—nearly every hospital guards its maternity center in this way. They must because children are unspeakably valuable, so much so that there are people who would steal them given half a chance. Locked doors and security cameras offer a much-needed layer of protection. They also testify to our universal recognition of the inestimable worth of children. But then there is legalized abortion. Like a bank that carefully locks the front door at the end of the workday but deliberately leaves the back door wide open, some hospitals work tirelessly to protect babies on one floor while quietly killing them on another. What a wicked world we've created.

Those of us who advocate for the unborn cannot comprehend how abortion supporters–many who are otherwise caring and compassionate people–can gaze adoringly at an ultrasound image of a developing baby sucking her thumb in utero and yet still deny her personhood and right to life. Nancy Pearcey responds to this curious phenomenon by stating "You are witnessing the power of a worldview."[2]

This seductive worldview is noxious indeed. But what is even more astonishing and infinitely more troubling is the number of Christians who also acknowledge the personhood of the unborn child yet still manage to remain emotionally unmoved by abortion's destructive storm.

Positionally, they may be quick to recognize the moral wrongness of abortion, but practically speaking, they feel nothing for the unborn. Rather than embracing and loving them as their neighbors, in many cases, they are in fact embarrassed of them, and treat them as modern-day lepers to be avoided.

In the movie *The Count of Monte Cristo*, a young merchant sailor, Edmond Dantes, is betrayed by his best friend who unjustly accuses him of committing treason. As a result, Edmond is declared guilty in the court of law and, as punishment, is consigned to Château d'If, the notorious island prison in the Bay of Marseille in Southeastern France.

Upon his arrival, he desperately argues his innocence before the sadistic warden, Armand Dorleac:

Edmond: Monsieur, I know you must hear this a great deal; I assure you I am innocent. Everyone must say that, I know, but I truly am.

Dorleac: Innocent?

Edmond: Yes.

Dorleac: I know. I really do know.

Edmond: You mock me?

Dorleac: No, my dear Dantes. I know perfectly well that you are innocent. Why else would you be here? If you were truly guilty, there are a hundred prisons in France where they would lock you away. But Château d'If is where they put the ones they're ashamed of.[3]

The French authorities knew Dantes was innocent but sacrificed him for political expediency. This painful scene reminds me of how ashamed our society has become of certain innocent children. The injustice done to Dantes, if understood by the French people, would have embarrassed and condemned his accusers. It is for this same reason that aborted babies are ushered out the back doors of abortion clinics and some of our hospitals never to be spoken of in public.

The children we value—the ones we're proud of—are protected by laws, locks, and security cameras. They're fawned over, smothered in kisses, and photographed endlessly. The only way out of the hospital for these cherished ones is through the front doors, safely cradled in their mothers' protective arms. The rest—the ones we're ashamed of—are quietly shipped out the back door in biohazard waste disposal bags, made to disappear into the dark night of incinerators and pathology labs. Otherwise, their lifeless bodies would shed light on the evil actions of the abortionist who dismembered them and on those who wax eloquently about "reproductive justice." Curious, isn't it? The very industry that encourages post-abortive women to "Shout Your Abortion!" will go to any length to conceal the mutilated bodies of their victims to attempt to dispose of their own guilt and shame.

Yes, the abortionist and his allies want their victims to go away, far away.

PASS THE BISCUITS, PLEASE

Sadly, so do many churches. It is not only the abortionist and his supporters who are ashamed of these little ones. Many Christians are too, which is why so few churches defend them, or even pray for them publicly. Much of the Church has assumed a ho-hum, "pass the biscuits please" attitude toward the unborn. When describing some of his colleagues in the academy, American political scientist Hadley Arkes could have been describing many of today's pastors; "They are people of large natures, with sensitivities cultivated to the most exacting liberal temper, and so they're prepared to engage their sympathies for all species of hurts suffered by the mass of mankind."[4] When it comes to speaking up for politically-approved victim groups they display "the most generous reflexes." For they know that when they do, they will be revered along with the heroic likes of celebrities such as Bono and Angelina Jolie. Yet when it comes to summoning sympathy for the unborn, the most victimized people on the planet, their moral reflexes become paralyzed, and their hearts turn to stone.

But it is not just many of our churches that have turned a blind eye to the unborn; many of our bible colleges and seminaries have as well. Conservative journalist and author George Will stated, "There is nothing so vulgar left in the human experience for which we cannot fly in some professor from somewhere to justify it." Tragically, universities that want to justify the unspeakably vulgar practice of abortion no longer must fly these professors in from somewhere else to do so; they are now on nearly every university campus in America, including many of our own Christian colleges.

I was once invited to speak at an event by an influential Christian leader known for his devotion to Christ and his love for people. The event emphasis was not a pro-life theme per se but focused on trusting God through times of pain and suffering. A few days before I was scheduled to speak, this man asked for a bio he could use to introduce me. I provided a short paragraph that focused mostly on my family and my pastoral background. But one sentence read: "Mike has a burden to awaken the Church to the plight of young mothers facing unplanned pregnancies and to the little ones they carry." This was hardly a sentence needing to be disinfected. However, when introducing me he read my bio verbatim but replaced that sentence with, "Mike saves lives." Noble sounding, perhaps, but life jackets and smoke alarms save lives too. Why the obscurity? Immediately following the event, he privately commended me for my pro-life work; yet publicly he was unwilling to associate himself with abortion's victims. I am quite confident that if my ministry was rescuing children from sex-traffickers (a vital ministry all Christians should support), this Christian leader would not have felt the need to scrub that detail from my bio. No, only the unborn are treated with such contempt.

THE HUE AND SHAPE OF OUR CHARACTER

In his autobiography, *My Bondage, My Freedom*, Frederick Douglass wrote of the "infernal character of slavery," and pointed out that: "The slaveholder as well as the slave is the victim of the slave system. A man's character greatly takes its hue and shape from the form and color of things about him." Abortion is like that. It has an "infernal character" about it that, when left unopposed, slowly plunders the conscience of the Church, leaving Christians cold and indifferent toward the "least of these." To borrow Douglass's words, the "hue and shape" of their character is being taken from the "form and color" of abortion. Failure to respond to the evil injustice of abortion with unyielding conviction and loving compassion is amputating our spirit and disfiguring the soul of the Church. It is damaging our gospel witness. After all, what is a watching world to think of Christians who speak adoringly of Jesus, the lover and protector of children, but who do not love the children He loves enough to protect them from being killed?

When it comes to how the unborn are viewed in our society, silent pastors and dispassionate Christians have a great deal in common with the abortionist: both view unborn children as miserably inconvenient. For the abortionist, this provides the justification to dismember them. For many pastors and churches, this provides the justification to do absolutely nothing while the abortionist dismembers them.

Could the lion-taming, justice-loving heroes of Hebrews 11 have imagined a day when shepherds called by God to protect the flock would instead surrender these precious lambs from their own flocks to the abortionist's knife without so much as a whimper from their pulpits? To lose the ability to empathize with helpless children who are being killed is to die on the inside.

WHEN GOOD MEN DO NOTHING

English statesman, Edmund Burke, famously quipped, "The only thing necessary for the triumph of evil is for good men to do nothing." I love the sentiment, but Burke's statement forces us to ask the obvious question: Do those who stand by idly in the face of evil deserve to be called *good*? Shouldn't this word be reserved only for those who, when confronted with the opportunity to intervene, risk their own comfort and safety to do so? As my experience with Manslow, detailed in the introduction, taught me, "innocent bystanders" are not always innocent, and they are not always good either. When given the chance, good men and women do not shirk moral responsibility. They do something; they speak, they act, they protect.

With respect to abortion, pulpit silence demonstrates the painful truth that each generation has the astonishing ability to be repulsed by the moral crimes of those who came before them while repeating many of those same offenses. For instance, we look back now with greater moral clarity at slavery and segregation in America and we scorn the memory of those whose apathy and love for personal comfort constricted their circle of moral responsibility so tightly as to exclude their black brothers and sisters. And yet millions of professing Christians give no thought to excluding unborn children from their circle of moral responsibility, or even voting for political candidates who vow to use their political capital to deny the unborn their most basic human right.

Comfortably removed by nearly 150 years from slavery and sixty years from segregation, it is easy to romanticize how we might have responded to the cruel and ruthless oppression of our black brothers and sisters had we lived then. Perhaps like me, you have wondered if you would have marched with them on the Edmund Pettus Bridge on March 7, 1965. We all like to imagine we would have. But remember, those brave men and women paid a heavy price for their principled stand. At the hands of Alabama State troopers, they were met with tear gas, night sticks, and fire hoses. That day is remembered as Bloody Sunday for a reason. None of us can know for sure what we would have done in 1965, but history has an annoying way of repeating itself and elective abortion now confronts us with a similar moral character test. Here is what we can know with certainty; if we won't stand for the unborn today while the cost to do so remains relatively low, we can be sure we would not have stood with our black brothers and sisters when the cost was so exceedingly high.

LIFE UNWORTHY OF MENTION

It is criminal that precious unborn children cannot find safe refuge in many of our churches. But if we will not love them as our neighbors, can we not at least find it in our hearts to love them as our enemies? Think of it, Jesus commands us to love our enemies, to do good to them, and to pray for them. Pastors and churches that are too ashamed to even pray publicly for the unborn have in essence declared them unworthy of meeting even the low threshold of "enemy" status. Whereas the Nazi designation for Jews was *Lebensunwertes Leben*, or "life unworthy of life," for these churches the unspoken designation for the unborn seems to be "life unworthy of mention," given the fact that they are not even prayed for.

To close off our hearts toward helpless children in their most desperate hour is to close off our hearts to Christ Himself. Jesus said, "I tell you that what you did not do for one of the least of these you did not do for me."[5] Being bound to Jesus Christ and the gospel doesn't provide refuge from the conflict over abortion; it demands our engagement.

It also demands our broken and contrite hearts.

CHAPTER 9
DID GOD REALLY SAY THAT?
THE BIBLE, ABORTION, AND WHOOPI'S FAULTY ASSUMPTION

Those who are determined to defend the indefensible are often driven to bizarre lengths to do so. Nowhere is this truer than when people try to defend the heinous act of abortion.

For example, the weird analogies and highly imaginative thought experiments invented by prominent pro-abortion philosophers intended to make the case for the moral permissibility of abortion are often so outrageous they prove more useful in exposing the moral weakness of their position.[1]

That said, however, defenders of abortion never show themselves more desperate or more debased than when they appeal to the Bible to try to justify abortion.

Unfortunately, most people, including many professing Christians, are uninformed with respect to what the Bible teaches about prenatal human life. Pro-abortion opportunists have seized on this ignorance, making sitting ducks of the unborn and further eroding the Church's influence in the battle for life.

Hoping to clear up some of this confusion, I want to respond briefly to five false claims regarding what the Bible teaches about abortion:

FALSE CLAIM #1: "THE BIBLE IS SILENT ON THE SUBJECT OF ABORTION."

Actress and comedian Whoopi Goldberg is adored for her long and distinguished career. A gifted entertainer, her roles in films like "The Color Purple," "Sister Act," and "Ghost" have elevated her to a near goddess stature in our culture. When Whoopi speaks people listen. Whoopi also just happens to be an unrelenting crusader for abortion.

While discussing the subject of abortion and the Bible on the TV show, *The View*, Whoopi proclaimed, "There's nothing in the book [the Bible] that says anything about abortion. Let's make sure of that. The Ten Commandments are the Ten Commandments, there's only ten."[2]

Whoopi's bold claim raises a question many people, and even many Christians, have quietly pondered; if abortion is so wrong, why doesn't the Bible mention it? For many pastors and professing Christians, the Bible's alleged silence on abortion justifies their silence.

Strictly speaking, Whoopi is correct; nowhere does the Bible mention the word "abortion" or even refer to the act of abortion. But Whoopi wrongly assumes that what the Bible does not explicitly condemn it therefore condones. This is absurd, and yet many make this mistake.

In an interview with *Rolling Stone Magazine*, former presidential candidate Mayor Pete Buttigieg criticized Christians by quoting pro-abortion pastor, William J. Barber, who accuses Christians of saying "so much about what Christ says so little about, and so little about what he says so much about."[3] Abortion supporters extolled Buttigieg for his sage-like insight.

But his comment ignores the obvious; there are many evils the Bible does not explicitly condemn such as joining the Ku Klux Klan and operating a child sex-trafficking ring. Are we to assume God sanctions these actions?

Of course not. We know God condemns these grave moral wrongs by *inference*. Given the fact that the Bible writers repeatedly speak of the inestimable value of all human beings, regardless of age, race, or gender, and given the fact that Jesus condemns harming children in the strongest possible terms, we know Jesus condemns these acts as well.

We don't need a Bible verse explicitly denouncing these baneful activities to know that they are sinful. Nor do we need a Bible verse explicitly condemning abortion to know that God abhors abortion. To suggest that the Author of Life, who warned it would be better to have a millstone tied around one's neck and be drowned in the sea than to harm a child would sanction the murder of unborn children is beyond profane.

When considering the alleged silence of the Bible with respect to abortion, it is important to remember that abortion is simply a method of murdering innocent human beings. As stated in chapter five, evil men and women throughout the centuries have devised innumerable devices and ways to kill each other.

Tragically, if the Bible expressly condemned by name every method of murder mankind has invented it would be thicker than the IRS tax code and would be too heavy to carry to church. Furthermore, with the ever-growing list of abortion methods and techniques it would be outdated before the ink dried (not that God's Word could ever be outdated).

Simply put, we do not need the Bible to prohibit by name each method of murder. Defending abortion based on the Bible's alleged silence is like defending the practice of beating the elderly to death by arguing that the Bible never mentions baseball bats. Murder by baseball bat is not more grievous to God than murder by guns or knives because it is not ultimately the *method* of murder that grieves the heart of God, but the murder itself.

Because the Bible clearly and repeatedly condemns the unjust shedding of human blood, we can know with certainty that God condemns murdering the elderly, regardless of how it is done. Likewise, we do not need a Bible verse specifically condemning abortion to know God condemns murdering the unborn.

So too, just as the Bible does not condemn by name every imaginable method of murder, neither does it single out particular classes of human beings that should not be murdered. For instance, the Bible never states, "Thou shall not murder toddlers" or, "Thou shall not murder people born in February."

Since we know every human being is a member of the species homo sapiens, and that human life begins at conception, we do not need a commandment declaring, "Thou shall not murder unborn children." The sixth commandment, "Thou shall not murder" is a protective commandment intended to benefit every human being, at every stage of development, wherever they happen to be located.

Now some might still object. In the absence of an overt biblical declaration stating, "The human fetus is a person," we might be accused of assuming too much with respect to the personhood of the embryo or fetus.

But although the Bible does not purport to be a primer on human embryology, the Biblical record is clear regarding the moral status of the unborn. Centuries before human embryologists understood the scientific facts of human reproduction, both the Old and New Testament writers, writing under the inspiration of the Holy Spirit, viewed the unborn child as a whole human person. This fact is often conveniently ignored by two specific groups: those seeking biblical justification to kill the unborn and those seeking biblical justification to do nothing as the unborn are being killed.

Approximately 700 years before Jesus entered time and space as an embryo in Mary's womb, Isaiah prophesied, "Therefore, the Lord himself will give you a sign: The virgin will be with child and will give birth to a son and will call him Immanuel."[4] Immanuel means "God with us." After the fulfillment of this striking prophecy, John wrote of Jesus, "The Word became flesh and made His dwelling among us."[5] This is the mystery and the miracle of the Incarnation; Christ did not become flesh at His birth, but at His conception. Since this is so, how can Christians marvel at the Incarnation and yet remain unconvinced of the full humanity or full personhood of the embryo or fetus? Are we to believe that the embryo inside Mary's womb was only a "potential person" and therefore only a "potential Son of God?" If so, what is so special about the Incarnation? Moreover, how can Christians who claim to accept the full humanity of the embryo or fetus remain so unmoved by the violence done to them by abortion? To marvel at the Incarnation while being indifferent to abortion's victims is like worshipping Christ while siding with Herod.

In the New Testament, Luke records a powerful exchange that takes place when Mary visits the home of Zechariah and Elizabeth. Both Mary and Elizabeth are pregnant. In Mary's womb, Jesus is just days or weeks old. John the Baptist ("John the fetus" as Greg Koukl refers to him at this stage of his development) is late into his second trimester in Elizabeth's womb. At this point John would have dwarfed Jesus in size, likely weighing about three pounds, with Jesus weighing only grams. Yet Luke writes, "When Elizabeth heard Mary's greeting, the baby leaped in her womb . . ."[6] A few verses later, Elizabeth exclaims, "As soon as the sound of your greeting reached my ears, the baby in my womb leaped for joy."[7] The word translated "baby," comes from the Greek word, *brephos* (βρέφος), which is used consistently by the New Testament writers to refer to babies born and unborn. Both Luke and Elizabeth proclaim that John, the embryo, is a "baby." Such a claim rejects the notion offered by those who argue that an embryo inside a woman is merely a "potential person" and not an actual person. Whether born or unborn, babies are babies.

Of course, we shouldn't be surprised when non-Christians find such biblical evidence for the personhood of the unborn child uninspiring. However, as Christians we ought to find this evidence not only convincing but motivating. What ought to concern us is not whether the Bible mentions the method of murder that we call abortion, but whether the Bible condemns murder, which it clearly does. As early as Genesis 9:6, we read, "Whoever sheds human blood, by humans shall their blood be shed; for in the image of God has God made mankind." The 6th commandment is unequivocal; "Thou shalt not murder."[8] In Proverbs 6:16-17, we read, "There are six things the Lord hates, seven that are detestable to him." One of those is "hands that shed innocent blood."

During the Greco-Roman period the people of Israel and Judah were burning their sons and daughters in sacrifice to the false god, Molech. The Lord became angry over this and said that to do so was to "profane the name of your God."[9] He further declared that any Israelite or alien living in Israel who did so must be put to death.[10] So vile was this abomination that God held even those who refused to intervene guilty:

> "If the people of the community close their eyes when that man
> gives one of his children to Molech and they fail to put him to death,
> I will set my face against that man and his family and will cut off

from their people both him and all who follow him in prostituting themselves to Molech."[11]

This demonic practice of feeding one's children to the fires of Molech is also condemned in Deuteronomy 18:10-13, 2 Kings 16:3 and 21:6, and Ezekiel 20:26, 31 and 23:37. And so, rather than being silent, the Bible repeatedly and unambiguously condemns murdering innocent children.

In the end, those who claim that the Bible is silent about abortion are either ignorant of what the Bible teaches or are determined to blame God for their moral indifference.

FALSE CLAIM #2: "EXODUS 21:22-24 JUSTIFIES ABORTION BY ASCRIBING A LESSER PENALTY FOR KILLING AN UNBORN CHILD THAN FOR KILLING A MOTHER."

Even though the bible writers consistently treat the unborn as persons, some quote Exodus 21:22-24, insisting this passage proves the unborn are not fully human since the penalty for accidentally killing a fetus is only a fine, whereas killing the mother is punishable by death. They appeal to the Revised Standard Version (RSV) translation, which reads:

"When men strive together, and hurt a woman with child, so that there is a miscarriage, and yet no harm follows, the one who hurt her shall be fined, according as the woman's husband shall lay upon him; and he shall pay as the judges determine. If any harm follows, then you shall give life for life, eye for eye, tooth for tooth, hand for hand, foot for foot . . ."[12]

There are serious problems with this view.

First, and most importantly, this argument rests on a less-than-convincing translation of the Hebrew word, "YATSA", which means "to emerge" or "come forth." This word appears in the Old Testament well over a hundred times and almost always refers to the emergence of a living thing.[13]

Whereas the RSV translates "YATSA" to read, "miscarriage," the NIV, NKJV, and NASB translate the word, "gives birth prematurely." In other words, the child was born alive and "no harm" followed.

In this case, since the child was not injured the penalty was merely a fine. "But if there is serious injury," presumably to either the mother or the child, the penalty is "life for life." The above-mentioned translations convey that both the mother and the child are covered by *lex talionis*, the law of retribution, clearly indicating that the mother and her unborn child are equal in value and dignity.

The second thing to note is that even if a lesser penalty is being ascribed for killing an unborn child than for harming the mother it doesn't follow that the unborn are not fully human or that a mother may intentionally abort her unborn child.

How could a passage that ostensibly addresses the accidental killing of an unborn child provide justification for intentionally killing an unborn child?

Finally, the earlier verses (vs. 20-21) speak of a master who unintentionally kills his slave while beating him. In this case the master escapes with an unstated punishment, but if the slave lives the master is not punished at all.

To conclude from this that the Bible considers slaves sub-human creatures who can be beaten with impunity is obscene and ignores the clear and consistent teaching of Scripture which says all humans have inestimable worth and should be treated with dignity and respect.

FALSE CLAIM #3: "NUMBERS 5:11-31 PRESCRIBES ABORTION."

This difficult passage spells out a strange ritual for husbands in ancient Israel who suspected their wives of adultery but lacked proof. The passage instructs the suspicious husband to bring his wife to the priest who would mix a cocktail of holy water and dust from the tabernacle floor. She was to drink it and if innocent, no harm would come to her.

However, if she had acted unfaithfully toward her husband the New International Version (2011) says that "her abdomen will swell" and "her womb will miscarry," which has led some to claim that the Bible prescribes abortion. In response, it should be noted that the NIV (2011) is one of the few translations that renders verse 22, as "her womb will miscarry." Neither the NIV (1984), the NASB, the KJV, nor the ESV make any mention of miscarriage.

Instead, each of these translates this verse similarly to the NIV (1984), which reads, "so that your abdomen swells and your thigh wastes away." This passage says absolutely nothing about miscarriage, abortion, or even pregnancy. Furthermore, the blessing of future fertility for the innocent wife suggests that the curse may have been bareness, not miscarriage or abortion. Again, if the woman is guilty, her abdomen will swell, and her thigh will waste away. But if innocent, "she shall be free and shall conceive children." That she would be free to conceive children suggests a child had not been conceived, which would mean an abortion had not occurred.

But even if the Hebrew language did refer to a miscarriage, this passage would do nothing to justify abortion. A natural reading of the passage suggests that the curse was from God, and not from the priest. Therefore, the child would have died because God decreed it, not because the priest gave her an abortifacient. God has the right to take human life, we do not.

God punished King David for killing Uriah and for committing adultery with his wife, Bathsheba, by striking his infant son dead after he had been born. But no one takes this to mean that parents have the right to take the life of their newborns.

FALSE CLAIM #4: "GENESIS 2:7 PROVES HUMAN LIFE DOES NOT BEGIN UNTIL A CHILD DRAWS HER FIRST BREATH."

Another popular attempt to weaponize the Bible to justify abortion, or to at least excuse one's moral indifference over abortion, is the often-repeated "breath of life" argument taken from Genesis 2:7, which reads:

> "The LORD God formed the man from the dust of the ground and breathed into his nostrils the breath of life, and the man became a living being."

Proponents of this view point out that Adam didn't become a living soul or "person" until God breathed into him the "breath of life" through his nostrils. They argue that since the unborn don't breathe air through their nostrils, they are not valuable human beings.

But many newborns don't breathe through their nostrils until a couple of minutes after birth. Are parents justified in killing their newborn children before they draw their first breath?

This passage is not offered as a biological lesson on human embryology. Rather, it is merely intended to provide an account of how God created Adam, the first man.

It describes when and how Adam came to life, but it does not describe when and how we came to life. Clearly none of us were fashioned in the way Adam was.

Furthermore, the developing unborn child breathes through the umbilical cord long before birth. Therefore, with respect to the child's breathing, the only thing that changes at birth is his or her *mode* of breathing.

FALSE CLAIM #5: "LEVITICUS 17:11 SAYS 'LIFE IS IN THE BLOOD.' SINCE EARLY EMBRYOS DO NOT PRODUCE BLOOD, THEY ARE NOT VALUABLE HUMAN BEINGS."

Leviticus 17:11 reads, "For the life of a creature is in the blood." From this verse, some abortion supporters conclude that since the embryo doesn't produce blood until about the third week, the embryo isn't a person, rendering abortion morally permissible at this early stage of development. Although most women do not know they are pregnant until at least 5 weeks, this would still render chemical abortions such as RU-486 and so-called emergency contraceptives morally permissible since the embryo would be killed before he or she begins producing blood.

But again, as with the "breath of life" passage, the purpose of Leviticus 17:11 is not to make a biological point, but rather a theological one. God uses blood here as a metaphor for life as He speaks to the Israelites about the sacrificial system that He had established for them. As others have pointed out, having blood doesn't necessarily make one alive and not having it doesn't necessarily render one dead. A fresh human corpse still has blood in it for a time but is clearly not alive. Conversely, mollusks and jellyfish don't produce blood, yet they are alive.

In conclusion, twisting and torturing the scriptures for personal gain is not new. In Genesis 3 the serpent visited Adam and Eve in the garden and whispered into their ears a seemingly innocuous question, but one designed to impugn God's character and to undermine His Word; "Did God really say . . . ?"[14] Centuries later, Peter wrote in his second epistle of "ignorant and unstable" people who distort Paul's letters, "to their own destruction, as they do the other Scriptures."[15] Isaiah warned, "Woe to those who call evil good and good evil, who put darkness for light and light for darkness, who put bitter for sweet and sweet for bitter!"[16]

No, the Bible is not silent on aborting innocent unborn children. Nor is it silent regarding our moral duty to those whose lives are threatened by such a godless and gruesome end. At a bare minimum, we can safely draw from Christ's command, "Do not hinder the children to come to me," that precious unborn children should not be denied the Church's best efforts to defend their God-given right to life, liberty, and the pursuit of happiness. God holds us morally responsible to protect the weak and vulnerable, and administering justice begins in the womb.

Make no mistake, the Bible is loud and clear about that.

CHAPTER 10

OBSTACLES, HURDLES, AND HITCHES

When animals kill each other, we do not say they have committed murder. Or when the neighbor's dog jumps the fence and impregnates our dog, we do not call the police to report a rape, no matter how unhappy we might be about the prospects of caring for a litter of pups. We understand that animals are ruled merely by instinct.

But it is the grandeur of human beings, God's image-bearers, to deny ourselves, to live ethically, and to make moral choices that benefit others which lifts us above the beasts. This grandeur is on highest display when these things are done to benefit the weakest and most vulnerable among us.

Of course, rising to the challenge requires us to think beyond the thin reasoning and paltry excuses that for five decades have obstructed the road to justice for the unborn.

In this chapter I will respond to six common excuses for the Church's silence that facilitate the rising body count of abortion and inflict untold damage on our gospel witness.

EXCUSE #1: "ABORTION IS A POLITICAL ISSUE. THE CHURCH SHOULD STAY OUT OF POLITICS."

Perhaps no argument has done more to paralyze the Church's influence than this. While many outside the Church believe abortion is merely a religious issue, some within the Church view it as merely a political issue. What both groups have in common is that they would like Christians to stop caring about and speaking up for the victims of abortion.

In response, there is no denying that abortion has become a political issue. However, abortion is more accurately described as a moral issue that has been *politicized*. But nearly every moral issue is eventually politicized, including war, slavery, and in recent years, marriage. Are these moral issues off-limits too?

If so, pastors like Dietrich Bonhoeffer, Charles Finney, and Vernon Johns who railed against the persecution of Jews, slavery, and Jim Crow laws were guilty of sticking their noses where they didn't belong. In countries like Iran and North Korea the gospel itself has been politicized and pastors who declare it are imprisoned and executed. Do they sin when they refuse to be silenced?

The apostles answered this question for us. When ordered by the Sanhedrin to stop preaching Christ, Peter and John responded, "Judge for yourselves whether it is right in God's sight to obey you rather than God."[1]

To be clear, pastors should protect their churches from evolving into political machines. Placing our hope in sinful politicians and in temporary political solutions rather than in God is idolatry. To do so also ignores our deepest need which is internal, not external. Author Michael Horton wisely states,

"Political solutions are not ultimate for the same reason medical solutions are not ultimate. In the end, we all die from something. That does not mean that we ignore the symptoms, nor that we refuse to follow the doctor's instructions and do what we can to remain alive, but it does mean that we do not treat them as the answer to life's greatest questions."[2]

The psalmist said it even better, "No king is saved by the size of his army; no warrior escapes by his great strength. A horse is a vain hope for deliverance; despite all its great strength it cannot save . . ."[3] Like horses, politicians are a vain hope for deliverance. This is so because our greatest enemy is within and only Christ can save us from ourselves.

However, it doesn't follow from this that the political realm should be roped off from our influence. Dutch theologian, Abraham Kuyper, famously wrote, "There is not a square inch in the whole domain of our human existence over which Christ, who is Sovereign over all, does not cry, Mine!"[4] Jesus Christ is Lord over all. Paul tells us, "All things have been put under his feet."[5] John describes Jesus as "King of Kings and Lord of Lords."[6] As Christians, we accept that Christ has a rightful claim over every aspect of our lives. He is Lord of our marriages, our singleness, our parenting, our careers, and Lord of our politics no less. Pastors teach us how to love our spouses, raise our children, behave sexually, and manage our money. They should also teach us how to vote. Love for our unborn neighbors demands that we use our political influence to make their lives better, or at least possible. For this reason, the pastor has a duty to teach biblical principles to his flock, so they might discern how to best use their vote to honor God and to protect their neighbors from harm.

On a related note, as pro-lifers, we are sometimes criticized by our own brothers and sisters in Christ for being single-issue voters simply because we refuse to vote for a politician or political party that denies the unborn their right to life. This criticism misses the point. Thoughtful Christians care deeply about many issues. But most pro-lifers view the legal destruction of unborn children as *the single most important issue*, and one that should be given greater moral weight when deciding which candidate or political party to support.

EXCUSE #2: "THE CHURCH SHOULD JUST PRAY ABOUT ABORTION."

This excuse may sound spiritual, but if thousands of toddlers were being killed legally every day–many from our own churches, would we think we should just pray about it? Would anyone judge this an adequate response? If your granddaughter was scheduled to die by abortion tomorrow morning, would you think you had done enough by merely praying for her? Would we esteem and celebrate the righteous Gentiles of the Holocaust if their only response to the persecution of their Jewish neighbors was to pray for them? Surely, God had called them and now calls us to do more. This is not evidence of a low view of prayer, rather, it is the acknowledgment that we are called to pray *and to act* on behalf of those being led away to slaughter.[7]

It has been my observation that those who argue we should just pray about abortion are usually the last ones willing to do so, at least not publicly. Sadly, the guidelines for creating a public prayer list are established in many churches by fear and a commitment to self-interest. Even in churches that claim to be pro-life, those most in need of prayer–the unborn–are frequently deemed unworthy of being prayed for publicly, even though such blatant disregard for children is condemned by our Lord. What does it reveal about our understanding of the gospel when praying for the unborn and offering help to their young parents does not fit with our philosophy of ministry?

So, if your church leadership argues, "We should just pray about abortion," kindly respond, "Great, can we start this Sunday? Will you lead us in asking God to turn the hearts of parents to their children and to lead us to these abandoned ones, so we might love them?"

EXCUSE #3: "ABORTION IS A WOMEN'S ISSUE. MEN HAVE NO RIGHT TO SPEAK UP."

Pro-life men are frequently lectured by pro-choice women (and curiously, by some pro-choice men) that since they cannot become pregnant, they have no right to express an opinion on abortion. That this conversation-stopper is never used to silence pro-choice men shows that the real complaint is not that men hold opinions about abortion, but rather that some men are thought to hold the *wrong* opinion. These men, we are told, must never be allowed to speak. Their opinions must not be tolerated.

This brand of thinking, springing from *Critical Theory*, is washing over our culture like a tsunami. It argues that the lived experiences of oppressed (or seemingly oppressed) people groups grant them privileged access to truth. Rational thought and objective facts count for nothing; the only thing that matters are the personal "lived experiences" of favored classes of oppressed people groups. As authors Margaret Anderson and Patricia Collins contend in their book, *Race, Class & Gender: Intersections and Inequalities*, "the idea that objectivity is best reached through rational thought is a specifically western and masculine way of thinking."[8] This irrational and poisonous perspective has influenced many abortion supporters to believe the lived experience of women (the oppressed) gives them access to truth that is unavailable to men (the oppressors). Since men don't have uteruses, they couldn't possibly add anything meaningful to the discussion. When they speak against abortion, they only show themselves to be card-carrying members of the tyrannical patriarchy, hell-bent on protecting their ill-gotten power.

But regardless of how our pro-choice opponents try to disguise it, disqualifying nearly half the U.S. population from speaking about abortion because of their gender is nothing short of sexist. As a pro-life man, the validity of my arguments against abortion are neither weakened nor strengthened by my anatomy. In fact, pro-life women use the same arguments as pro-life men. As Francis Beckwith points out, "Arguments don't have genders, people do."[9]

The *"No uterus? No opinion!"* crowd has successfully used this ploy to dupe even many shepherds, into self-censoring when it comes to defending the unborn. But since abortion unjustly kills human beings, it cannot be properly understood as a women's rights issue. It must be understood as a human rights issue. This means that men, and pastors in particular, have not only a right to speak in defense of the unborn, but they also have a moral obligation to do so. This is not patriarchal oppression speaking; this is common sense.

Consider the shocking story of 28-year-old Catherine "Kitty" Genovese who was brutally raped and stabbed to death outside her apartment in Queens, New York, on March 13, 1964. Two weeks later the *New York Times* reported, "For more than half an hour . . . 38 respectable, law-abiding citizens in Queens watched a killer stalk and stab a woman in three separate attacks in Kew Gardens."[10] One man allegedly witnessed the attack and phoned his girlfriend for advice on what to do. She advised him not to get involved, so he didn't. The details of the *New York Times'* reporting of this account have since been called into serious question and the number of heartless spectators appears to have been wildly exaggerated. Nonetheless, the original report outraged Americans and Kitty's story will forever be associated with terminal indifference, spineless complicity, and societal decay.

Although it is abhorrent to think anyone would have ignored Kitty's cries for help, we are justifiably more appalled at the thought of men having done so. This is because men are generally physically stronger than women and we expect them to use their strength to protect women from harm. After all, even radical feminists, if honest, are for good reason more outraged over a man who beats his wife than over a woman who beats her husband. Both are bad, but we all recognize that men should be the primary protectors of the weak and vulnerable, and that should apply whether the assailant is a rapist or an abortionist.

Therefore, the charge that men have no right to speak against abortion is not merely an attack on pro-life men; it is an attack on masculinity. Gentlemen, we must not allow ourselves to be intimidated into silence by those who despise us and wish to emasculate us by insisting we do nothing to defend helpless children from abortion. For if they succeed, we will find that we have become the despicable cowards our critics thought us to be.

EXCUSE #4: "BUT AT LEAST ABORTED CHILDREN GO TO HEAVEN."

This cringeworthy assertion is made by two kinds of people. First, there are those who want to justify abortion by using Christian theology as a cudgel against the unborn and against those who defend them. They argue, "Aborted babies never have a chance to grow up and reject Christ. Therefore, according to Christian theology, since the aborted go to heaven, abortion is the best way to save souls. We do them a favor by sending them to a better place." A second group that employs this calloused argument includes Christians who want to justify their own apathy toward the unborn. This rationalization for abortion is flawed for at least three reasons.

First, it is presumptuous. While there are good reasons to believe aborted babies (as well as babies that are miscarried and the severely developmentally disabled) go to heaven, the Bible does not expressly state this.

Second, if we are to view abortion as "mercy killing," as this view seems to suggest, wouldn't this also serve as an argument for killing children who have been born? It turns the villainous King Herod into an angel of mercy for having ordered the slaughter of all boys two-years-old and younger in Bethlehem.

Finally, God commands us to "rescue those being led away to death," not stand by as they are being killed. Nowhere does the Bible allow, and much less prescribe, killing precious human beings to prevent them from sinning and thereby sealing their fates in hell. God's only plan for redeeming sinful humans is through the atoning sacrifice of Christ's death on the cross. Those who adopt such a reprehensible "salvation-by-dismemberment" evangelism strategy should check themselves for a moral pulse.

EXCUSE #5: "SPEAKING OUT AGAINST ABORTION WILL TURN PEOPLE AWAY FROM THE GOSPEL."

No, it won't. In fact, preaching against abortion, or any sin for that matter, is precisely what turns people to the gospel. As Paul wrote, "I would not have known what sin was had it not been for the law. For I would not have known what coveting really was if the law had not said, 'You shall not covet.'"[11] The truthfulness of this passage has been proven by the countless heartwarming testimonies of men and women who after being confronted with the sin of abortion have found salvation and freedom in Christ as a result. Pro-life speaker and author, Stephanie Gray Connors states, "Our culture as a whole, and each of us individually, are desperately in need of being healed from the sin of abortion. But we will not be healed until we are forgiven, and we will not be forgiven until we repent, and we will not repent until we acknowledge there's a need to repent."[12] She is right, and this happens when Christians and pastors speak truthfully about the sin of abortion.

To believe that preaching against abortion turns people away from the gospel reveals a lack of confidence in the power of the gospel and of the Holy Spirit to convict and draw sinners to the One who "hath shed his own blood for our souls."[13] In reality, it is the refusal to speak against the sin of abortion that keeps people separated from the gospel. Those who do not acknowledge their sinful, helpless condition will never acknowledge their need for Christ's saving grace.

Suppose we applied this same mentality to other sins. Does preaching against the sin of adultery turn adulterers away from the gospel? Was John the Baptist responsible for turning Herod away from the gospel when he confronted him over his adulterous affair with Herodias? With the likely exceptions of Herod and Herodias, does anyone really believe John should have remained silent?

The church that refuses to stand against the sin of abortion has already abandoned the gospel they claim to be protecting. The gospel demands that we love our neighbor as ourselves, but we cannot love our neighbor if we refuse to act when someone has a knife to his throat. The great heroes of the Christian faith understood this. Randy Alcorn writes,

"John Wesley actively opposed slavery. Charles Finney had a major role in the illegal Underground Railroad. D. L. Moody opened homes for underprivileged girls, rescuing them from exploitation. Charles Spurgeon built homes to help care for elderly women and to rescue orphans from the streets of London. Amy Carmichael intervened for sexually exploited girls in India, rescuing them from temple prostitution . . . There is no conflict between the gospel and social concern."[14]

To abandon the unborn is to abandon the gospel itself. With respect to preaching against abortion, the pastor's obligation is not to try to predict how someone might possibly respond so he can tailor his sermon in such a way as to guarantee no offense is taken. Instead, he is to "speak the truth in love"[15] and trust God's Spirit to convict and draw people to Himself.

EXCUSE #6: "PRO-LIFERS ARE ANGRY, VIOLENT TYPES. I DON'T WANT TO BE ASSOCIATED WITH THEM."

Even good and noble causes tend to attract a small number of strange, obnoxious, or even malevolent people. This was true for the civil rights movement, the women's suffrage movement, and regrettably, this has been true for the pro-life movement too. Unfortunately, it only takes a few to spoil a movement's reputation and thereby injure its mission. However, if the cause is lucky enough to enjoy the support of a sympathetic media, you won't even hear about the bad apples.

Of course, the pro-life movement is not so lucky. We routinely suffer grossly unfair treatment at the hands of the mainstream media, which serves as Big Abortion's ministry of propaganda. Our nation's newsrooms are a united front in their support for abortion.

On the rare occasion that a pro-lifer speaks or acts in a way that is foolish or worse, the story is looped for days, thereby cementing in the minds of millions of Americans that pro-lifers are unhinged crazy people.

But the unfair treatment we receive is not merely the result of media bias, it is the result of media corruption. It is a deliberate ignoring or twisting of a story to malign pro-lifers and to protect legalized abortion. Volumes of evidence could be cited, but consider again the media's refusal to report on the murder trial of abortionist Kermit Gosnell. Brian Clowes writes:

"His case had everything the media usually loves: A repulsive main character who is the most prolific serial killer in the nation's history and a major drug dealer, a disgusting 'House of Horrors,' a nest of racketeers, massive government corruption . . . But in this case, since Gosnell was an abortionist, the mainstream media did its absolute best to cover up the trial and pretend that it never took place."[16]

When pressure from pro-lifers eventually goaded some in the media to grudgingly provide scant coverage of the trial, *HuffPost Live* host Marc Lamont Hill confessed,

"For what it's worth, I do think that those of us on the left have made a decision not to cover this trial because we worry that it'll compromise abortion rights. Whether you agree with abortion or not, I do think there's a direct connection between the media's failure to cover this and our own political commitments on the left."[17]

The *Washington Post's* Melinda Henneberger wrote, "I say we didn't write more because the only abortion story most outlets ever cover in the news pages is every single threat or perceived threat to abortion rights."[18] Years earlier, NARAL Pro-Choice America's Susanne Millsaps dared to state the obvious, "The media has been our best friend in this fight. They claim objectivity, but I know they're all pro-choice."[19] In their effort to guard against every perceived threat to legalized abortion, media pundits often brand pro-lifers as "extremists," "violent fanatics," and "hostile to women's rights."[20]

In truth, most pro-life advocates are reasonable, kind-hearted, peaceful people. I know because I have the privilege of meeting thousands of them each year. They are humble, unassuming moms and dads, grandmas and grandpas, and children who devote their time, talents, and treasure to defend the unborn and to provide for women. Of course, the sacrificial efforts of these gentle lambs never make the news. It has been my experience that the loathsome behavior or physical violence that does occasionally occur at pro-life demonstrations or prayer vigils is almost always done by abortion-rights supporters or abortion clinic staff. If these incidents are reported at all, they are generally spun in such a way as to shift the blame onto pro-lifers. I have witnessed pro-choice students and protestors who have physically attacked pro-lifers, stolen pro-life signs, and vandalized pro-life displays, often with impunity.

Unlike our pro-choice counterparts, pro-life organizations condemn violence in all forms. The pro-lifers I encounter are embarrassed by, and ashamed of, the small number of pro-lifers who speak or act in ways that dishonor God and play into the hands of our adversaries, damaging our witness. We naturally, and rightfully, feel the desire to distance ourselves from them. At the same time, however, we need to be careful not to throw the baby out with the bathwater. It's absurd to assume that a small number of obnoxious pro-lifers might somehow exempt us from the responsibility of protecting the weakest members of the human family from the deadly threat of abortion.

Finally, it is interesting that in His parable of the Good Samaritan Jesus doesn't reveal the motivations for the priest's and the Levite's decision to ignore the man who was beaten and left to die. Perhaps this is because any reason they might have offered would be unworthy of mention since there is no excuse for ignoring victims in ditches or in wombs. For this reason, we dare not blame our inaction on the bad behavior of others. As James admonishes us, "Anyone, then, who knows the good he ought to do and doesn't do it, sins."[21]

CHAPTER 11
UNMUTING THE PULPIT
AND UNLEASHING THE GOSPEL

"Why doesn't my pastor talk about abortion?"

It was an honest question, but one that sounded more like a stinging indictment. I had just addressed a high school assembly about abortion at an evangelical Christian school in a large city.

During the assembly, I had presented a case for the humanity and personhood of the unborn child and had introduced my audience to the video mentioned in chapter three, which showed abortion's victims. Now I was in classrooms for the remainder of the day, fielding questions and responding to challenges.

As the class began, I made a few introductory comments and then invited students to ask questions. The first question came from a senior girl whose hand shot up like a rocket. With a puzzled look and a tone of disgust that was palpable, she asked, "Why doesn't my pastor talk about abortion?"

It was clear that this was the first time she had been confronted with the truth about abortion and now she felt betrayed by her pastor's silence on such an important issue. If only her pastor–and every silent pastor–could have witnessed her sense of betrayal. Her pointed question was ultimately one that only her pastor could have answered but based her response I doubt any answer would have satisfied her.

This high school student isn't alone in feeling betrayed. I frequently encounter others like her who are mystified over and deeply troubled by their pastors' silence on abortion. For many pro-lifers, respect for pastoral leadership is severely diminished by disappointment and disillusionment over their shepherds' refusal to give voice to the voiceless. Reluctant to cast their pastors in a negative light, they frequently soften their complaints by saying something like, "My pastor is a really good guy, but . . ." and then they go on to express frustration over his silence.

What is in question is not whether hushed pastors can be "good guys," but whether they can remain silent and be *good shepherds*. Jesus minced no words when he answered this question for us. He called the shepherd who does not protect the sheep a "hireling," or hired hand. When the hireling sees the wolf coming, he "flees because he is a hireling and does not care about the sheep."[1] Deaf to the cries of the unborn lambs under his pastoral care, the muted pastor surrenders vulnerable children, potentially from his own flock to Planned Parenthood and her bloodthirsty allies. God spoke strong words through the prophet Ezekiel to self-serving shepherds: "This is what the Sovereign Lord says: Woe to you shepherds of Israel who only take care of yourselves! Should not shepherds take care of the flock?"[2] Jude describes them as "shepherds who feed only themselves."[3]

Thankfully, there are pastors who joyfully accept their pastoral duty to guard the flock. I am privileged to meet some of these compassionate and courageous shepherds in my work. But sadly, in far too many churches it is the sheep, and not the shepherds, who lead this charge. Although the pro-life movement continues to grow in size and effectiveness, it's my observation that this is in spite of pastors and not because of them. While the civil rights movement was led largely by pastors, the pro-life movement is led almost entirely without them. To make matters worse, not only are the vast majority of pastors not leading in the battle for life, few are even following. In fact, in many cases these insubordinate gatekeepers have effectively bolted the doors of their churches, locking the pro-life message out altogether.

A charitable spirit might incline some to conclude pastoral silence over abortion does not necessarily point to cowardice or apathy, but to feelings of inadequacy in not knowing how to address the subject biblically. It is true, few seminaries prepare up-and-coming pastors to teach a biblical view of human dignity or inspire them to become courageous life defenders. But in a day when nearly everyone is talking about abortion, when science has settled the question of when human life begins, and when a plethora of helpful pro-life resources are so easily accessible, pulpit silence is indefensible.

Although refusing to do anything meaningful to defend the unborn under their pastoral care, many of these shepherds claim to be pro-life. Practically speaking, however, this simply means they "don't like abortion." Their opposition to the legal killing of unborn children is about as consequential as one's opposition to eating brussels sprouts. At best, it affects only themselves. Their involvement, if it can be called that, is only as spectators. They enjoy the comfort of watching the battle over abortion from the safe seats high in the bleachers, free from the pain and inconvenience of actual engage-ment. As Gregg Cunningham says, "Most people who say they oppose abortion do just enough to salve the conscience but not enough to stop the killing."[4] And when a pastor's only interest is in salving his conscience, not much salve is required.

For example, some pastors feel they have done their part by

simply attending the local pregnancy center banquet, or by granting the center's director ten minutes one Sunday in January to share from his otherwise muted pulpit. In this way, he cracks the door of his church open just enough to assuage his guilt and to provide cover from those who might dare to ask why he cares so little for the ones for whom Christ cares so deeply.

God sees through this. Patronizing pro-life gestures leave the unborn in his flock vulnerable to those who would profit from their blood, and it leaves those who have had abortions to suffer silently in their guilt and shame.

Merely disliking abortion hardly qualifies one as a pro-life pastor. So, what does it mean to be a truly pro-life pastor in an abortion culture? What does ministry faithfulness look like? Let me share four fundamental duties of the faithful pro-life pastor.

DUTY #1: THE PASTOR MUST LEAD THE CONGREGATION IN PUBLIC PRAYER FOR THE UNBORN AND FOR THEIR PARENTS.

James assures us that "the prayer of a righteous man is powerful and effective."[5] God promises to hear and to respond to the prayers of His people. What we pray for in our churches reveals what we value, and ultimately, what we believe God values.

Paul admonished the Ephesian believers to, "be alert and always keep on praying for all the Lord's people."[6] The pro-life pastor understands that "praying for all the Lord's people" includes praying for the unborn. Unashamed of these helpless little ones and their parents, he humbly leads his flock in public prayer, pleading with God to use his congregation to bring an end to abortion.

It is often pointed out that praying for our enemies comes with the personal benefit of having our own hearts softened toward them.

Praying for the unborn has the same effect. If we want our churches to become rescue missions for the unborn and for young couples facing unplanned pregnancies, we must begin by asking God to break our hearts for what breaks His.

I once spoke to a large gathering of pastors in Dallas, Texas. Before my talk, I was approached by a respected pastor of one of the largest churches in that city. I was struck by his compassion for the unborn.

During our brief conversation, he shared that his church regularly and publicly prays for the unborn and for their parents. In addition, they publish an invitation each Sunday in their bulletin to those who may be facing unplanned pregnancies.

A few days after returning home from this trip, I became more curious about the content of his invitation and so I contacted his office to request a copy. It reads,

"Welcome to Park Cities Presbyterian Church. We are glad you joined us today. We want to come alongside you in hospitality and prayer. At the conclusion of our services, there are men and women at the front and back of the sanctuary to meet and pray with you–in complete confidence. If you are experiencing an unplanned pregnancy, you are loved. For support, please call us or call Thrive Women's Clinic at (phone number) or Kari (last name and phone number)."

What a beautiful expression of the gospel! And what an encouragement to know there are pastors who are unashamed of the unborn and their parents. This simple, yet powerful invitation to receive prayer goes a long way in nurturing a culture for life and establishing a safe community for the hurting.

DUTY #2: THE PASTOR MUST TEACH THE CONGREGA-
TION ABOUT HUMAN DIGNITY AND EQUALITY, SO THEY
CAN ENGAGE THE CULTURE EFFECTIVELY.

Those under our pastoral care live and travel in a world that says there is nothing special or exceptional about us as humans.

Atheist Richard Dawkins argues that we are nothing more than chemically sophisticated "survival machines-blindly programmed to preserve" what he refers to as "the selfish gene."[7] Atheist Lawrence Krauss opines, "We're just a bit of pollution; if you get rid of us . . . the universe would be largely the same. We're completely irrelevant."[8]

According to this view, we are nothing more than our brains, a mere collection of cells. We have no immaterial soul, no objective value or purpose, and no future beyond the grave.

This dismal worldview led American author and social critic, Camille Paglia, to write in her book, *Vamps & Tramps*, "Fate, not God, has given us this flesh. We have absolute claims to our bodies and may do with them as we see fit."[9] In this kind of world, the only guiding ethic is what makes me happy or what feels good. A survival of the fittest culture emerges; we justify killing our own offspring and killing our own parents if they stand in the way of our happiness.

One-hit wonders, Denny Zager and Rick Evans, in their gloomy 1968 hit song, "In the Year 2525," imagined a day when scientific technology would catastrophically outpace mankind's morality. One verse predicted, "In the year 6565, ain't gonna need no husband, won't need no wife. You'll pick your son, pick your daughter too, from the bottom of a long glass tube." That day is already upon us as technological advances continue to push the ethics envelope with bioethical challenges such as human cloning, embryonic stem cell research, so-called "after-birth abortion," and euthanasia. The biblical doctrine of the Imago Dei, once almost universally accepted, which holds that we are God's image-bearers who are "worth more than many sparrows," is now castigated as "speciesism"[10] on university campuses.

If not Christians, who will restore moral sense and order to this scene? Yet, few Christians have been trained to respond to the flawed philosophical underpinnings of such a seductive and pervasive world-view. A lack of doctrinal vigilance from the pulpit and a spirit of cultural retreatism in many churches have left some Christians questioning the relevance of their own faith. Furthermore, a growing number of non-Christians dismiss Christianity as little more than pixie-dust religion. Christian philosopher and apologist, William Lane Craig responds to this crisis,

> "If Christians could be trained to provide solid evidence for what they believe and good answers to unbelievers' questions and objections, then the perception of Christians would slowly change. Christians would be seen as thoughtful people to be taken seriously rather than as emotional fanatics or buffoons. The gospel would be a real alternative for people to embrace."[11]

To accept this challenge, pastors must train their congregations to defend the biblical position that every human being has inestimable worth and deserves legal protection at every stage of development. Doing so is a faith builder for our congregations. When Christians are taught a biblical view of human dignity and are equipped to defend the sacredness of human life, they begin to see how their faith connects with real life issues. This inspires them to share their faith with greater confidence and demonstrates to non-Christians the relevance and truthfulness of the gospel. After all, if we have something compelling to say about weighty moral issues like abortion and euthanasia, perhaps we have something important to say about matters of forgiveness and eternity, too.

Having trained thousands of adults and students at conferences, in churches, and in Christian schools, I can attest to the fact that those in our congregations need and want this kind of training. They soak it in like human sponges. Thankfully, there is no shortage of popular level pro-life apologetic resources–books, videos, and pro-life speakers–to help pastors provide this training for their flocks. A list of excellent resources is available in the appendix.

In the end, the pastor who equips his congregation with pro-life training is not merely contending for the unborn, he is contending for Christianity itself.

DUTY #3: FROM HIS PULPIT, THE PASTOR MUST CONDEMN ABORTION IN NO UNCERTAIN TERMS FOR THE EVIL THAT IT IS.

The pro-life pastor loves children, and therefore hates abortion. He sees the legalized murder of innocent children by abortion as the defining moral issue of the day, an affront to divine authority and a full-frontal assault on the flock under his care. He is deeply offended by abortion and his protective anger burns within. Unlike many of his colleagues who haughtily dismiss God's command to "speak up for those who have no voice"[12] as a distraction from the gospel, the pro-life pastor sees his response to abortion as the gospel in action. He gladly accepts his pastoral duty to protect the whole flock, even those yet to be born.

Like the apostles and the Old Testament prophets, the pro-life pastor's preaching is disruptive in the best sense. He stirs the conscience of his flock by pressing the question, "Is our gospel for everyone or only for those it is convenient to love and protect?" The passion and conviction with which he asks this question provides the answer, and no one in his congregation is left wondering where he and God stand on the matter. He's not merely pro-life, he's unabashedly *anti-abortion*. He doesn't stutter or stammer or tiptoe around the abortion issue by speaking only in safe and flowery terms of the "preciousness of life." Instead, he preaches boldly against the Goliath of abortion with the prophetic fire and conviction of a man whose heavenly mandate compels him to compel others. He is eager to support his local pregnancy care center, but he knows that attending pro-life banquets and sponsoring baby-bottle drives is no substitute for bold, biblical preaching that condemns abortion and champions the cause of the little ones Christ loves so tenderly.

Let me address two common objections to this challenge to boldly condemn abortion. First, many pastors believe a "seeker sensitive" ministry approach exempts them from obeying the command to "speak up for those who have no voice." One must question the merits of a ministry philosophy that prevents shepherds from protecting their sheep. Furthermore, we must ask, if people are seeking the truth, why are so many seeker-sensitive churches hiding it from them, especially on a matter with such dire consequences? The apostle Paul set the parameters for true seeker-sensitive ministry when he wrote, "For I have not hesitated to proclaim to you the whole will of God."[13] In the end, withholding truth from those who seek it is cruel, not sensitive.

Second, some pastors believe that division over abortion is the reason to avoid the subject altogether. Sadly, congregational division over abortion is not uncommon. Churches are often divided in this way and to make matters worse, such division is frequently found along political party lines. For this reason, pastors are often reluctant to approach the subject out of fear that doing so could bring this division to the surface. Such reluctance may arise from a pastor's sincere concern for the flock and a genuine desire to maintain peace, but it is badly mistaken. When a congregation is divided over abortion, avoiding the subject does not protect unity; it protects division.

Such division may reveal more about the pastor than it does about his flock. Something has gone horribly wrong when a congregation cannot agree that killing unborn children is morally reprehensible. The pastor who presides over such a divided family should ask himself, "Why is my flock divided over such a foundational moral issue?"

The truly pro-life pastor doesn't exploit congregational division over abortion as a convenient excuse to remain silent. Instead, resolving such division becomes his calling. He meets this challenge with the wisdom of Christ and with all the passion of a reformer until he has chased from the minds of his people every trace of moral confusion and every hint of discrimination, and until they can say with one united voice, "from now on we regard no one from a worldly point of view."[14]

Haman the Agagite in the Old Testament book of Esther was consumed with hatred for the Jews. His genocidal plans for God's chosen people presented Queen Esther with a serious moral dilemma: approach King Xerxes uninvited and risk her own life to save her people or remain silent to save herself. The pastor whose church is divided over abortion is confronted with a similar dilemma with respect to abortion's victims, but with far fewer risks: speak up for the unborn to save them from abortion or remain silent to maintain personal comfort. As was true for Esther, the pastor who speaks and acts on behalf of the unborn stands to gain much more than he could ever lose. Jesus said, "Whatever you did for one of the least of these brothers of mine, you did for me."[15] There can be no greater reward for pulpit faithfulness.

A faithful pastor, aware of his duty to his flock, at the same time embraces his duty to those outside the church. His righteous preaching, which lays bare the evil of child killing, reverberates beyond the walls of the church, so that all will know "a prophet has been among them."[16] His unflinching conviction resurrects the spirit and passion of Frederick Douglass, who, when confronting apathy over slavery, wrote,

> "For it is not light that is needed, but fire; it is not the gentle shower, but thunder. We need the storm, the whirlwind, and the earthquake. The feeling of the nation must be quickened; the conscience of the nation must be roused; the propriety of the nation must be startled; the hypocrisy of the nation must be exposed; and its crimes against God and man must be proclaimed and denounced."[17]

DUTY #4: THE PASTOR MUST LEAD THOSE WHO'VE HAD ABORTIONS TO THE ONE WHO DIED TO FORGIVE THEM.

The same pastor sees no conflict between loving innocent unborn children and loving guilty adults. By "speaking truth in love"[18] he does both. Convinced that the sin of abortion is no match for the grace of God, he is not stingy with the gospel. He preaches hope and forgiveness through the spilled blood of Christ for those who've spilled the blood of the unborn. He delights in pointing those who have aborted their children to the One who promises, "When the Son sets you free, you will be free indeed."[19] He cannot imagine hiding such hope from those burdened by the sin of abortion. The Good News is like a fire shut up in his bones; he cannot keep it in. His teaching and counseling ministry nurture a community where love and compassion are in full supply, where abortion becomes unthinkable, and where sinners find real forgiveness and freedom from guilt and shame.

Conventional wisdom says broaching such an unpleasant subject runs the risk of dredging up painful memories and inflicting greater injury on those who have had abortions or have been responsible for them. Such a notion is built on the assumption that time heals all wounds. It doesn't. It also assumes that the healing process is automatically underway. It isn't. Time, at most, deadens the conscience and numbs the pain. Only Christ can heal the soul. Only Christ can forgive and make new. Preaching about the sin of abortion and the forgiveness offered to the guilty doesn't interrupt the healing process, it helps it to begin.

The pastor who chooses silence over faithfulness communicates one of two destructive messages: either abortion is not so bad, or the gospel is not so good (or both).

Let's consider the first regrettable message of pastoral silence: *abortion is not so bad.* When the pastor remains silent, those in his congregation who have aborted their children, or may be considering doing so, are left to conclude, "My pastor speaks out against the sins of gossip, slander, and adultery, but feels no compulsion to speak out against abortion. It must not be a big deal." In this case, his silence communicates indifference at best and approval at worst, paving the way for more babies to die by abortion.

The second regrettable message of pastoral silence, *the gospel is not so good,* leaves others to conclude, "The sin of abortion is so bad that my pastor can't even mention it. My sin must be unforgivable." In this case silence communicates condemnation with no hope of forgiveness. The pastor's refusal to confront the sin of abortion undermines the sufficiency of Christ's atoning work on the cross by signifying that Christ's blood is an inadequate remedy for this sin. This silence further alienates those who regret their abortions, leaving them no hope of escape from the cold and lonely prison of guilt and shame. But ironically, it is only when abortion is exposed as sin and confessed as such that forgiveness becomes possible; "Godly sorrow brings repentance that leads to salvation and leaves no regret."[20]

Scott Klusendorf explains that pastoral silence "does not spare post-abortion men and women guilt–it spares them healing."[21] He's right. Abortion is evil because it kills precious unborn children, but the soul-cleansing gospel of Jesus Christ is beautiful because it provides forgiveness for guilty adults. Christ calls pastors to thunder from their pulpits both the sin of abortion and the grace of God. The pastor who fails to fulfill either of these obligations fails to love as Christ has called him to love.

In the end, every pastor who claims to be pro-life must contend with the question, "Is the gospel the remedy for all sin, or only for those sins that are comfortably exposed?" Either our gospel will positively impact our response to unborn children and to those who have had abortions, or our failure to respond will negatively impact our gospel witness.

A WORD TO PASTORS

If you are a pastor, these guidelines will help you preach powerfully and effectively about abortion:

1. Determine to fear God more than men. Pray for greater courage. Remember, love is not self-seeking, and it always protects. Paul wrote to Timothy, "We have not been given a spirit of timidity, but a spirit of power, of love and of self-discipline." [22]

2. Make the gospel the center of your preaching and teaching against abortion. The gospel is the best hope for those considering an abortion and the only remedy for those who have aborted their children.

3. As you prepare your sermon, ask yourself, "How would I approach this if toddlers in my flock were being legally killed? What amount of time and what level of urgency and passion would I devote to this?"
4. Preach as if your son or daughter is secretly bearing the guilt and shame of a past abortion.
5. Preach as if your unborn grandchild's life depends on it.

Finally, as a shepherd you are first and foremost a *sheep protector*. What an influential position you are called to. Like a fireman or an EMT, your preaching can directly save the lives of children and protect parents from aborting their children. Pastors who refuse to safeguard the unborn under their care disqualify themselves from serving in this important role. But good shepherds protect the weak from the strong, bring hope to the hopeless, and grow spiritually mature congregations.

CHAPTER 12
THE ART OF ARGUING WELL
WINNING THE ABORTION DEBATE WITHOUT LOSING YOUR OPPONENT

I met Reagan on a flight home from a speaking engagement. He sat across the aisle from me. I started a conversation by asking a few friendly questions and discovered that Reagan had married two years earlier, worked for the United States Air Force, and was returning from a business trip. We talked for about ten minutes before the plane departed, at which time we each opened books to read for the next hour or so of our flight.

About twenty minutes before our plane landed, I noticed Reagan had closed his book and so I asked another question or two. Eventually, Reagan asked about my work. I explained that I advocate for the unborn, as well as for their mothers facing unplanned pregnancies. Reagan was unfazed and without skipping a beat he responded, "I lean toward the pro-choice position. Tell me why I should be pro-life." I couldn't believe the golden opportunity before me. I answered, "Well, actually, you shouldn't be pro-life if human embryologists are wrong about the embryo." Reagan's curiosity piqued, and with this simple response I had launched us into a meaningful dialogue by focusing our discussion on the question at the heart of the abortion debate, "What are the unborn?" Before long, we had an audience as the passengers in the two rows in front of us didn't even pretend not to be listening. Those in the aisle seats had unashamedly repositioned themselves to better eavesdrop. Reagan's obvious comfort with our conversation, expressed by his many questions, provided me the opportunity to briefly make the case for life.

As the plane landed, I ended the conversation by thanking Reagan for the enjoyable conversation. At this point, most of the passengers crammed into the aisle and prepared to deplane. Reagan and I both remained seated waiting for the line to start moving and with our audience still within earshot Reagan surprised me with yet another direct question: "Thirty years of marriage, eh? What's your secret?" I marveled over the gift this exchange was and wondered if our little audience suspected Reagan and me of collusion. I answered, "Reagan, there's no secret. My wife and I are convinced Jesus Christ is who He claimed to be: God who became flesh to live a perfect, sinless life and to offer Himself as the sacrifice for our sins. We've built our lives on this truth and on His teachings and this has made all the difference in our marriage." Reagan accepted my answer and kindly thanked me. Along with the other passengers, we began to file out of the plane. I felt great emotion and thanked God for this encounter. I have no idea what lasting impact, if any, my words had on Reagan or on our extended audience. But God knows, and I trust Him to use my words for His purposes.

I have reflected on this meeting many times since, and I confess that this was a conversation I could not have had 20 years ago. At that time, I lacked both the knowledge and skill to navigate through thorny subjects like abortion without my passions getting the better of me and thereby bringing out the worst in my opponent. In my earlier years I meant well but I often walked away from conversations like this feeling defeated and guilty. Perhaps you can relate. It is possible to have the right answers and the right motivation but the wrong approach. The apostle Paul must have had this in mind when he encouraged the believers in Colossae, "Be wise in the way you act toward outsiders; make the most of every opportunity. Let your conversation be always full of grace, seasoned with salt so that you may know how to answer everyone."[1] To this end, let me share six simple strategies that will help you win the abortion debate without losing, or alienating, your opponent in the process.

STRATEGY #1: TAKE AN HONEST INTEREST IN OTHERS

With the noteworthy exception of public pro-life events and displays designed to create public dialogue, generally the most effective way to start one-on-one conversations about abortion is to talk about other things and simply look for natural openings. As with Reagan, I did not set out to have a conversation about abortion. However, by expressing an honest interest in his life and engaging him in friendly dialogue, a door of opportunity opened which allowed me to go places in our conversation where I might not have been permitted otherwise.

We often hear that people are tired of talking about abortion. This has not been my experience. I find that people are very interested in discussing abortion but are more inclined to do so when they know our care is genuine and not a sneaky sales tactic meant to bait the unsuspecting into conversations about our pet topic. Oftentimes the greatest obstacle to productive conversations about abortion is not the difficult nature of the subject itself, but the difficult nature of our own selfish hearts. If we are not careful, our burden for the unborn (or any theological, political, social, or moral topic) can blind us relationally, causing us to view family, friends, and strangers as targets to talk to about what interests us, rather than as people who should interest us.

Christian speaker and author John Lennox states, "Many of us are mono-maniacs when it comes to the Christian faith. That's all we can talk about, and people find us profoundly boring." To be clear, Lennox is not ashamed of the gospel or shy about sharing his faith. He does this often and well. But he makes an important point. We need to make our conversations about more than what interests us. He offers a simple but priceless piece of advice: "If you want people to be interested in your message, you be interested in them."[2] Few people do this better than Lennox. His warm, engaging personality is both disarming and inviting. While taking an interest in others seems to come naturally for him, this is a skill each of us can and should work to develop.

Developing this skill starts with asking, "Am I the kind of person who takes an interest in others? Do I ask others about their marriages, families, and careers? Or am I consumed with talking about myself and my interests? Am I truly interested in the opinions of others, or am I only interested in those who agree with me?" Effective conversations about sensitive subjects like abortion depend on trust. Showing sincere interest in others helps build this trust, and as my conversation with Reagan showed, this trust can be established even during brief encounters.

STRATEGY #2: ATTACK ARGUMENTS, NOT PEOPLE

Compassion is a hallmark virtue of the Christian life. The psalmist describes God as "compassionate, slow to anger and rich in love."[3] We frequently read in the gospels of Christ's compassion for lepers, prostitutes, and unscrupulous tax collectors. Even as He hung dying on the cross, Jesus prayed for his executioners, "Father forgive them for they know not what they do." Likewise, as His followers we are commanded to "clothe yourselves with compassion."[4] As stated in chapter two, broken people and beleaguered communities have bene-fitted richly throughout history from Christian compassion expressed in ways too numerous to count.

But there is one act of compassion that is often overlooked and even disparaged within the Christian community, and this is to the peril of our pro-life efforts: the art of arguing and arguing well. Now we don't tend to equate arguing with compassion. In fact, they seem like polar opposites. When we think of compassion, we envision feeding the poor or visiting those in nursing homes.

Arguing, on the other hand, conjures up images of angry people yelling at each other. But this is not the kind of arguing the apostle Peter had in mind when he wrote, "Always be prepared to give an answer to everyone who asks you for the hope that you have."[5]

The word "answer" comes from the Greek word apologia (ἀπολογία), from which we get the English word *apologetics*, which simply means an argument or a defense. Therefore, we could rightly translate Peter's words to read, "Always be prepared to give an *argument* for the hope that you have."

In this respect, we are to become arguers in the classical sense of the word, just as an attorney argues on behalf of a client, offering good reasons–or arguments–to prove his client's innocence. This means we must know about the physical and moral nature of the unborn child and about the immoral nature of abortion.

We must also be able to anticipate and respond to popular objec-tions our opponents will raise. If we lack this knowledge, we will be inclined to avoid the conversation altogether or to come out swinging in hope that an abundance of zeal will compensate for a lack of knowledge.

But the art of arguing well involves more than having right

answers to tough questions. Peter continues, "But do this with gentleness and respect." When an unborn child's life is imperiled by the beastly cruelty of abortion, she doesn't need a warm blanket or a hot meal; she needs an advocate armed with good arguments and a gracious manner, because if this act of compassion is unsuccessful, there won't be an opportunity to express another.

Of course, this presents us with a formidable challenge in an "I'm-just-looking-for-a-reason-to-take-offense" culture that now equates disagreement with bigoted intolerance. Anyone who dares to disagree with the pro-choice position is branded a "hater" and ironically, isn't tolerated. This kind of bullying censorship is having a chilling effect on moral and political discourse today, causing many Christians to run from conversations about abortion. But just as we are called to love the unborn, we are also called to love our pro-choice opponents. The late Supreme Court justice, Antonin Scalia, once quipped, "I attack ideas; I don't attack people. And some very good people have some very bad ideas. And if you can't separate the two you gotta get another day job."[6] Scalia makes a profoundly important point. We must resist the temptation to attack or demonize those with whom we disagree.

Preaching the gospel repeatedly brought Jesus' disciples face-to-face with hostile opponents. They undoubtedly felt the urge to lash out, to respond sarcastically, and to portray their antagonists unfairly. But they didn't. When speaking of Jesus and His teachings which animated their evangelistic efforts and governed interaction with their enemies Paul wrote, "Christ's love compels us, for we are convinced that one died for all . . ."[7] What a powerful example. Clever tactics and good apologetic arguments are vitally important but arguing well on behalf of the unborn must begin with love.

This isn't always easy. While Scalia was right in saying that some very good people have some very bad ideas, it is equally true that some very bad people have some very bad ideas too. As a result, like the first-century believers, we frequently find ourselves on hostile turf facing belligerent opponents. Their fanaticism for abortion "on demand and without apology" often results in bitter hatred for anyone who holds an opposing view. If we are motivated by anything less than Christ's love, the worst in them will bring out the worst in us.

However, loving, and respecting people does not mean loving and respecting their ideas or opinions. It is rightly said that while all men are created equal, all ideas are not. In fact, some ideas are so bad and so dangerous that we are duty-bound to expose and defeat them. If this sounds like an illicit ambition for the Christian, consider Paul's word to the church in Corinth: "We demolish arguments and every pretension that sets itself up against the knowledge of God, and we take captive every thought to make it obedient to Christ."[8] Like Antonin Scalia, Paul understood that defending good arguments sometimes involves demolishing bad ones. When an idea or argument justifies killing innocent human beings, defeating it becomes our calling.

While speaking on a university campus a few years ago, it dawned on me that some of the militant abortion activists I encountered there could have been unborn children whose lives I and many others fought for twenty years earlier. Now, as young adults they have turned on us by becoming impassioned advocates for the very evil that once threatened their own lives. This irony escapes their notice, but it should not escape ours. We must act lovingly toward all human beings, in and out of the womb, even when they act uncharitably (or worse) toward us. Jesus said, "If you love those who love you, what reward will you get? Do not even tax collectors do the same?"[9]

In the end, presenting solid arguments in a gentle and respectful manner is an act of compassion everyone can live with.

STRATEGY #3: DEFINE WINNING THE ABORTION
DEBATE FROM A BIBLICAL PERSPECTIVE

Everyone loves a winner: whether in sports, politics, or romance, we all want to win. But since the definition of "winning" is often confused by morally muddled opinions and ideologies, it is important to define it properly in the context of conversations about abortion.

First, winning does not necessarily mean having your pro-choice friend on his knees renouncing his pro-choice position and professing his newfound pro-life convictions. This flawed definition puts all the responsibility on you to change hearts and minds, erecting one more barrier to overcome. While we should contend for life with passion, there is freedom in recognizing that our part is simply to "make the most of every opportunity," to be sure our conversations are "always full of grace and seasoned with salt," and then to trust God for the results. Understanding this helps take the pressure off and allows our conversations to flow more naturally.

Furthermore, winning the abortion debate should never mean embarrassing our pro-choice opponent. We have all have seen social media posts promoting videos that boast, "Pro-Lifer Crushes Pro-Choicer!" and, "Christian Owns Atheist!" as if crushing and "owning" our fellow image-bearers is what Christ wants from us. Because the truth is on our side, defeating pro-abortion arguments isn't that difficult; almost anyone can memorize and regurgitate correct answers to tough questions. But pro-life apologetics is not an end in itself; it is the means to an end. We are to become skillful ambassadors, not apologetics junkies obsessed with stockpiling clever responses, so we can victoriously humiliate our pro-choice friends. Winning the abortion debate must be about more than winning arguments, it should always be about winning people.

This happens when good arguments are delivered with kindness and wisdom. Because we are often the last line of defense for mothers and their unborn children, we must become the kind of people with whom others want to talk and share openly. Treat your opponents in such a way that if they visit your church and sit in the pew next to you, you will have nothing for which to apologize.

My conversation with Reagan was a gift from God. Although he did not convert to a pro-life position during our conversation, I trust the Holy Spirit will continue to work in him, perhaps through others, to bring him to a knowledge of Christ and to the realization that every human being is precious and should be cherished and protected. If God used my efforts to cause Reagan (and those listening in on our conversation) to think more deeply about abortion, that is a win for each of us, and for the unborn.

STRATEGY #4: STAY FOCUSED ON THE UNBORN AND STAY OUT OF THE WEEDS

Perhaps you have noticed that abortion supporters want to talk about anything and everything except the unborn child. They talk about a woman's "right to choose," a broken foster-care system, hard-case scenarios like rape and incest, and a litany of other secondary issues. While these topics deserve our attention, none of them has anything to do with the moral question of abortion. Even though many pro-choice people would have us believe abortion is a complicated matter, the moral question of abortion is a simple one to answer. Scott Klusendorf lays out the pro-life argument with clarity:

Premise 1: It is morally wrong to intentionally kill an innocent human being.
Premise 2: Abortion intentionally kills an innocent human being.
Conclusion: Abortion is morally wrong.[10]

If the unborn child is a human being, as the second premise argues, then abortion is a moral wrong that every human being should be protected from.

When Reagan asked why he should be pro-life, I responded, "Well, actually, you shouldn't be pro-life if human embryologists are wrong about the embryo." By responding this way, I centered our discussion on the question at the heart of the abortion debate, "What is the unborn?" Framing the debate in this way wasn't a greasy tactical maneuver on my part; it was an honest effort to help Reagan think correctly about the moral question of abortion. By centering our discussion on the biological nature and full personhood of the unborn child (subjects addressed in chapters three and four), I was able to avoid the minefield of endless strawman arguments and exhausting bunny trails. As Greg Koukl states, "If the unborn are not human no justification for abortion is necessary. But if the unborn are human, no justification for abortion is adequate."[11]

So, keep the unborn child front-and-center in your conversations about abortion or you will end up in the tangled weeds of red herrings, empty slogans, and misleading clichés. And if that happens, everyone loses–especially the unborn child.

STRATEGY #5: WHEN APPROPRIATE, BE THE ONE TO END THE CONVERSATION

This may seem like an odd piece of advice, but we have all encountered well-intentioned pro-lifers whose zeal blinded them to normal social graces causing others to avoid them like the plague. Being the one to end the conversation in situations with family and friends where you are likely to have future opportunities to revisit the topic can be particularly helpful. When people know they are free to leave a conversation, they feel free to stay with it or to return to it at another time. That said, this may not be the advice I would give to a pregnancy care center counselor who is speaking with an abortion-minded client. In this case the urgency of the moment should dictate the length of the conversation.

Again, as was the case with Reagan, after several minutes of making my case and responding to his questions and challenges, I offered an end to the conversation (sure, the fact that our plane landed helped this along), however, it became clear he wanted to continue to talk. Although we were discussing a subject over which we disagreed, Reagan wasn't looking for a parachute or the emergency exit. He saw me as genuinely interested in him and in his views on abortion. He knew I could talk about other things beside myself and abortion. He also knew he was free to leave the conversation, which made him feel free to pursue it, granting me even greater opportunity.

STRATEGY #6: KEEP IN MIND THAT THE WORLD IS WATCHING YOU

We've all heard the boast, "I don't care what anyone thinks of me!" Often, this is said admiringly of others; "Joe is his own man. He couldn't care less what people think of him!" And sometimes we hear fellow Christians say something like, "I don't care what others think about me. I only care about what Jesus thinks about me." But there is no place in the Christian life for not caring what others think about us. Although we shouldn't be consumed with an unhealthy need to be liked or accepted (Mark Harrington, president of the pro-life ministry, Created Equal, reminds us, "Successful reformers are rarely liked, while liked reformers are rarely successful"[12]), we should nevertheless care deeply about how we are perceived. Paul reminds us that we are not our own, that we have been "bought at a price."[13] We represent another King and another Kingdom: "We are Christ's ambassadors as though God were making His appeal through us."[14] When it comes to conversations about abortion, what we say and how we say it can have life and death consequences for our tiniest neighbors. This should cause us to be on our best behavior, "so that in every way" we "will make the teaching about God our Savior attractive."[15]

If we want to be heard, it helps to be likeable. Unfortunately, many of our adversaries have painted us as belligerent, religious know-nothings bent on oppressing women. We have had this narrative–this bad reputation–pressed onto us. But with a little wisdom and humility, we can overcome it. Whether speaking face-to-face or interacting on social media with abortion supporters, when we rise above the low expectations set for us, we become a curiosity of sorts. This can go a long way in setting the right tone for conversation. It soon became clear during my conversation with Reagan that he was not my only customer. The attentiveness with which our fellow passengers watched and listened suggested this may have been the first time they had encountered rational pro-life arguments presented in a respectful manner.

Much of our public discourse over morality and politics has decayed into a snarky game of "gotcha" where civility and diplomacy are sacrificed on the altar of winning at all costs. But the command to "Make the most of every opportunity" is not about scoring points or crushing people; it is about finding ways to argue our case persuasively, with kindness. Remember, "Gracious words are a honeycomb, sweet to the soul and healing to the bones."[16] Jesus said, "Out of the overflow of the heart" the "mouth speaks."[17] To be sure that our words are "sweet to the soul" we should ask ourselves, "What is in my heart? Do I value crushing my enemies more than winning them over?"

Proverbs 25:11 tells us, "Like apples of gold in settings of silver is a word spoken in right circumstances." A little kindness goes a long way in developing the type of trust that invites greater and more meaningful dialogue. So, when someone responds to your pro-life stance on social media in an uncharitable or an accusatory manner, consider beginning your response with, "Thank you Jenny for your comments. I value the exchange of ideas and welcome your thoughts." Then, after answering her challenge, consider ending with, "Jenny, do you see this differently? I look forward to your response. Thanks again!"

Finally, as my conversation with Reagan demonstrated, and as I have argued in chapter ten, defending the unborn and sharing the gospel are not competing interests. Doing the first often presents the opportunity to do the second.

CHAPTER 13
RAISING THE RIGHT KIND OF REBELS

L ucy and Kali, students at the University of Florida, were
friendly enough when I approached their table display that
included a petition and t-shirts and stickers, which read, "Ban the 'R'
Word" and "Spread the Word to End the Word." The word in their
crosshairs was the word "retarded." I was on their campus for the
purpose of engaging students like Lucy and Kali about abortion.

They seemed pleased when I showed interest by asking, "Can you
tell me about your campaign?" Elaborating on the pain suffered by the
hurtful "R word," they spoke of their goal to convince the world to
stop using it, recommending the more sensitive label, "intellectually
disabled." After listening carefully to their concern and asking clari-
fying questions, I offered that I was the father of a daughter who is, as
they prefer to say, intellectually disabled. This seemed to buy me at
least a bit of credibility so I took the opportunity to explain that I had
come to their campus to expose a similar, but greater injustice;
namely, that our society actually targets "intellectually disabled"
unborn persons for death by abortion at an alarming rate.[1]

I soon discovered that Lucy and Kali considered themselves "pro-choice" and supported the practice of aborting the very people they wanted to protect from name-calling. This wasn't a big surprise since this kind of moral confusion is widespread on college campuses. I don't write this to be unkind; Lucy and Kali were gentle-spirited and otherwise bright college students. Yet here they were, lost in the thick fog of moral dissonance, justifying the legal extermination of the very people they were hoping to shield from offensive words.

We spoke for nearly 30 minutes during which time I attempted to expand the borders of their compassion by focusing on the nature of the unborn and on the question, "What makes humans valuable?" At one point I referenced the children's rhyme, "Sticks and stones may break my bones, but words can never hurt me." To the delight of these energetic crusaders, I pointed out that this popular rhyme ignores the fact that some words do hurt and hurt badly. But I also pointed out what should have been obvious to them; sticks and stones can impose an even greater harm than words, especially when the "sticks and stones" represent the abortionist's canula and suction machine, causing the death of an innocent child.

As I continued to make my case and to respond to their objections, Kali eventually ran out of arguments and conveniently found another passerby to speak with, leaving me with Lucy, who was more open to discussion. I got the distinct impression that she was hearing the case for life for the first time. The longer we spoke the more uncomfortable she appeared to be with her own position–one that condemns calling people names just because they have an intellectual disability, and yet defends brutally killing them for the same reason.

Lucy finally conceded–albeit reluctantly–that her position was inconsistent, but rather than humbly sending up the white flag of surrender, she dug in her heels and stated defiantly, "And I'm okay with that!" But it was clear that Lucy was not okay with it; she was visibly troubled by her own inconsistency. Human pride sometimes erects a thick wall that often takes time to come down, and Lucy just needed some time. As we ended our conversation, I thanked her for the cordial dialogue and encouraged her to give more thought to my challenge. She promised she would.

Although I find the worthiness of Lucy and Kali's moral crusade uninspiring, their earnest desire to make a difference is both admirable and revealing. God has placed this longing in each of us. The apostle Paul wrote, "For we are God's craftsmanship, created in Christ Jesus to do good works which God prepared in advance for us to do."[2] Doing good by rebelling against evil is in great measure what we were created for. But of all the injustices Lucy and Kali could have been rebelling against, attempting to ban a word was the best they could do. Again, I don't write this to disparage them; I genuinely pity them and so many like them who have traded in their birthright as God's image-bearers for virtue-signaling bandwagons. Now at least Lucy and Kali's cause–while lackluster in purpose–was peaceful. This cannot be said of many of their peers whose chosen campaigns of feigned moral outrage have resulted in the violent actions of setting fire to buildings, overturning police cars and attacking innocent people.

SYNTHETIC THRILLS AND LOW EXPECTATIONS

Teenage rebellion is nothing new. Since the beginning of time, teens have been rebelling against their parents, teachers, society, and God. When you take the normal adolescent craving for individualism and significance, mix in raging hormones, and corrupt it with a fallen nature, rebellion flows out as naturally as water from a spigot. Sadly, however, more often than not, the Church has proven woefully incapable of harnessing these primal urges for good. Because it is much easier to entertain our young people with synthetic thrills than to train them in godly, self-sacrificing character, we have deprived them of a calling worthy of their humanity. We have thought and expected too little of them. We have wrongly assumed that they cannot think wisely, care deeply, or act meaningfully about important issues like abortion. As a result, scores of young people like Lucy and Kali have become rebels without much of a cause, consigned to protest merely for the sake of protesting.

The American Church is producing a listless, shallow generation. Practically speaking, Jesus' call to deny ourselves, to take up our crosses and to follow Him has been filtered from their church experience. As a result, pledging their lives, their fortunes, and their sacred honor for the sake of Christ and for others seems absurd. Many of our teens read only what is found on a Twitter feed. They have become experts on pop-culture and can tell you everything you never wanted to know about the plastic lives of Hollywood celebrities, but they have never heard of Christian heroes and heroines like Hudson Taylor and Elisabeth Elliot and would find their stories dull if they did. Not unlike those outside of the Church, many of our own sons are squandering their lives glued to a computer screen vanquishing digital, make-believe villains and surfing porn sites but are incapable of fighting a real battle or committing to a real woman. They are ruled by feelings but feel nothing for others. They may be angry but know nothing of righteous indignation. Our daughters have not fared much better under ineffectual churches. The biblical warning, "charm is deceptive, and beauty is fleeting" is all but ignored, while the divine enticement, "but a woman who fears the Lord is to be praised" holds no allure. Instead, social media's hypnotic spell has them posing endlessly for the camera, obsessively consumed with the physical while starving the spiritual.

MEETING THE CHALLENGE

The pro-life movement is hitting this challenge head-on and thousands are responding. Caroline Bowes of Mossyrock, Washington, is a case in point. In 1996, her parents, Ted, and Robyn Bowes, had been struggling with infertility. To restore their natural ability to conceive they pursued medical care and soon discovered that they were pregnant with quadruplets. Given the high-risk nature of Robyn's pregnancy, the ultrasound tech thought she was doing them a favor when she handed them a business card for the local abortion clinic. Later, a physician at the fertility clinic as well as another high-risk pregnancy doctor suggested "selective reduction," an act they described as "eliminating" (codeword for *killing*) two of the "pregnancies" (codeword for *babies*) to increase the odds of survival for the remaining two siblings. However, despite serious physical risks to both Robyn and her unborn children, abortion was out of the question. She and Ted would continue to anchor their trust in the One who promises to go with us and to comfort us when we walk through the dark valley of death's shadow. God honored their commitment and on November 5, 1996, Robyn gave birth at 32 weeks. They named the smallest of the four Caroline, who weighed in at only 3 pounds, 5 ounces. Caroline's "womb mates," as she affectionately refers to her siblings, included two sisters and one badly outnumbered brother. Caroline's three siblings spent 3 weeks in the neonatal intensive care unit at Good Samaritan Hospital in Phoenix, Arizona. Caroline was the last to leave the hospital one week later.

I first met Caroline on the phone when she invited me to speak at a kick-off rally for a new 40 Days for Life campaign she was spearheading in her community. During our initial conversation, I was impressed by her gentle, but tenacious spirit. Months later we met in person when I travelled to Washington to speak at her event. Caroline is a petite, soft-spoken and compassionate young lady whose joyful spirit is contagious. The words she speaks are gracious and kind. To describe her as non-threatening is an understatement to say the least. But Caroline is a formidable foe to Washington's abortion industry. She follows in the spirit of Esther before the king–a gentle elbow of sorts to the pastors of her community.

Determined to engage the churches of her community, Caroline reached out by phone to twenty local pastors. Some didn't bother to return her call, but she persevered and was eventually granted meetings with half of them. As a result, seven pastors joined her to pray outside of their local Planned Parenthood clinic. But Caroline didn't stop there. The next year she continued to call on pastors. This time eleven of them joined her on the streets with sixteen churches participating in her campaign. This number continues to grow as Caroline continues to provide leadership. Caroline has also become the Director of Development at her local pregnancy resource center in Centralia, Washington. Caroline Bowes is a pro-life trailblazer.

The Justice Rides organized by Created Equal are another example of young people making an impact for life. Inspired by the legacy of the Freedom Rides of the civil rights movement, the Justice Rides are designed to provide students the opportunity to expose the age-based discrimination of abortion. These Justice Riders–high school and college-age students–are trained to make the case against abortion, including both what to say and how to say it. Next, they board buses, going on the road to create informed public dialogue about abortion. Traveling to college campuses and downtown squares, students stand alongside large images of aborted children in all three trimesters and kindly ask passersby: "What do you think about abortion?" Through this respectful, but deliberate approach, hundreds of students are given the opportunity to advocate for the lives of countless unborn children, and to share the gospel of Jesus Christ with men and women trapped in pain and guilt from previous abortions. I have participated in these Justice Rides and have watched these young lions of the faith confidently and graciously defend the cause of the unborn, often in the face of hostility. As they work to save and change the lives of others, they are having their own lives changed forever.

IF YOU SEE A GOOD FIGHT, GET IN IT!

A father in the early twentieth century once gave his son, Vernon Johns, some unusual advice. He told him, "Son, if you see a good fight, get in it!" Johns was born April 22, 1892, in Prince Edward County, Virginia. His grandfather, a black slave, was hanged for killing his master. His mother was the daughter of a slave who was routinely raped by her white slave owner. Johns would grow up to precede Martin Luther King Jr. as the pastor of the Dexter Avenue Baptist Church in Montgomery, Alabama. Although his name has been overshadowed by names like King and Rosa Parks, Johns is considered by many to be the father of the civil rights movement. His penetrating oratory skills and unwavering convictions laid the foundation for King and Parks and others who would later lead the charge against racial segregation. His powerful sermons with provocative titles such as, "It's Safe to Murder Negroes in Montgomery," and "When the Rapist Is White," drew no small amount of attention from the watchful eyes of the white racists of Montgomery, nor from his nervous congregation. Before Rosa Parks got the idea, Johns once refused to give up his seat to a white man on a Montgomery bus. When he was forced off the bus, he courageously demanded his fare back. Astonishingly, he got it. No doubt Vernon's father would have been proud to see that his godly counsel found fertile soil in the heart of his son and reaped such an abundant harvest for so many.

As Christians, we are to be the best of citizens. We keep our lawns mowed, we don't double park our cars and we say things like, "Yes, ma'am" and "No, sir." We fear God, we honor the king, and we render to Caesar that which belongs to Caesar. And we certainly don't go around picking fights. However, we should recognize a good fight when we see it, and the state-sanctioned war against defenseless unborn children by abortion is a good fight. Being the best of citizens demands that we roll up our sleeves and get into the ring. And the parental duty to disciple our children demands that we encourage them to roll up their sleeves and get into the ring, too. So, when we lead our children to stand, to pray, and to protest outside of America's abortion clinics, and when some of our sons grow up and become pastors who set their pulpits ablaze with courageous preaching that exposes abortion and champions the cause of the most orphaned among us, we are not picking a fight; we're merely responding to the fight that has come to us.

Parents and pastors who truly believe in the sanctity of human life in both the womb and in the classroom will work to instill within their young apprentices hearts of compassion and a love of justice for all. This should start when our children are still very young. A simple reading of Dr. Seuss's *Horton Hears a Who*, with its beautifully simple message, "A person's a person no matter how small," can be followed with a short lesson exposing the error of attaching human value to superficial distinctions such as one's size or location. Even small children can understand and appreciate this profoundly important truth. Additionally, how we treat babies, the elderly, the handicapped and those with different skin colors provide teachable moments for our children.

In the 90's I pastored a church in Fort Wayne, Indiana, that ministered to developmentally disabled adults. These brothers and sisters seasoned our church family in wonderful ways. One man, George, had been born with cerebral palsy, which severely arrested his cognitive skills as well as his physical mobility. George walked with a bad limp and the paralysis in his left arm forced his hand to draw up tight to his chest. As a result, George had a difficult time performing simple tasks. One winter morning after our church service ended, I glanced across the sanctuary to see my then 7-year-old daughter, Marisa, who had stood up on a chair so she could reach high enough to pull George's atrophied arm down to help him get his coat on. My heart was warmed as I watched this tender scene unfold. Even young children can develop hearts for the hurting and the oppressed.

Parents and pastors alike do well to remember that we cannot give away what we do not possess. I once spoke during a Sunday evening service at a small church about abortion. The pastor's wife, and not the pastor, had invited me in. Through my brief interactions with him leading up to the day I was to speak, it became clear that his wife possessed what he lacked: a heart for the unborn. As the evening ended, the pastor thanked me for coming, then attempted to excuse himself from his pastoral duty to the unborn by saying, "I'd love to speak against abortion in my church, but I'm afraid I would just break down and cry." Somehow it escaped his thinking that brokenness and empathy is precisely what both the unborn and his flock needed from him. Instead, a supposed fear of expressing emotion over the slaughter of unborn children provided the cover to say and do nothing. With this kind of soft pastoral leadership is it any mystery why so many of our young people find the Church boring and irrelevant? They understandably doubt a man who claims to be deeply moved over abortion and yet is content to remain silent. Shouldn't real brokenness have the opposite effect? Pretending to be too emotionally wrecked to preach against abortion does not reveal a broken heart: it reveals a selfish, cowardly heart. If the unborn could speak they could rightly ask, "With friends like this, who needs enemies?"

On this note, teaching our young people about the horror of abortion and our Christian duty to the unborn involves more than merely saying the right thing; they need to see and feel the depth of our emotion, our conviction, and our righteous indignation. Our burden over abortion should animate us and inspire them. Our message to our young people must be clear: abortion presents your generation with the greatest moral injustice the world has ever known, and you should do something about it. I have taken this message to thousands of high school students in classroom, auditorium, and church settings throughout the United States. Students are routinely exposed to guest speakers and no doubt many of these speakers are engaging and have important things to say. However, I am sometimes led to believe that at least some of the previous guest speakers and their topics have not managed to capture the attention of students. I occasionally overhear murmurs and grumblings as students file past me into the auditorium for the morning assembly unaware that I am the guest speaker. It seems low expectations for me are prebuilt into my captive audience. At best, they initially view my visit as little more than an escape from their normal school day routine. But within the first few minutes of my talk, all of that changes. The serious and relevant nature of abortion rivets their attention. When the light of truth exposes the evil injustice of abortion and students hear the pro-life position rationally and passionately defended the response is remarkable. I see this all the time. They are anything but bored. And when the challenge is put to them to take a stand by swimming upstream in the culture of death you can hear a pin drop, even in an auditorium of 1,000 students. They're listening because this subject matters to them.

Regardless of what side of the abortion debate students find themselves on, they feel something about abortion and want to express it. Even after a 50-minute talk, I almost always encounter students who hang around to interact further. Sometimes these are abortion supporters who have discovered a friendly opponent and want to put forth challenges. Oftentimes it is pro-life students who want to know more or want to express gratitude for my having given voice to their convictions. All of this is evidence of the important need that is being met. These students want and need to know how they can champion the cause of the unborn.

By introducing them to satisfying answers to our opponents' toughest challenges, we strengthen their faith, galvanize their convictions, and unleash them to rebel against the injustice of abortion. Unlike many of their predecessors in the now defunct "Occupy Wall Street" campaign of 2011, whose lofty convictions evaporated when the cold weather set in, driving them from their makeshift tents in Zuccotti Park and back into the warm, insulated cocoons of their parents' basements, the pro-life students I encounter are truly principled (and they shower regularly!). The pro-life movement has convinced thousands of young people that they can change the world by rescuing unborn children from certain death. Whereas those in the abortion industry see our young people as nothing more than advanced primates to be exploited for financial profit, those of us in the pro-life movement see them as rescuers in God's revolution called to a life of eternal significance. They are not rebels without a cause; they are passionately engaged in the defining moral cause of our time, and they're making a profound difference.

Barbara and I have never regretted the regular Thursday morning trips with our children to pray and protest outside our city's local abortion clinic. While the inside of an abortion clinic is the most dreadful place for children, the outside of the abortion clinic is the perfect place for them. It was there that our children witnessed first-hand the somber scenes of women and teenage girls entering the clinic to have their children aborted. They encountered the bitter hatred of pro-abortion clinic escorts and the vile invectives of abortionist Ulrich George Klopfer. They watched respected adults from our church family and from other churches contending for the lives of the unborn by praying for and counseling young abortion-minded couples. And they saw Christians pooling their money to help young mothers in need. As a result, their compassion for the weak and vulnerable began to blossom and their love for justice was stirred. They also learned to love and pray for their enemies. Over time, our burden–*Christ's burden*–for unborn children and their young mothers became theirs as well. Today, each of our children has a passion for the unborn and two of them have dedicated themselves to full-time pro-life work.

William Lane Craig states,

"It's insufficient for youth groups and Sunday school classes to focus on entertainment and simpering devotional thoughts. We've got to train our kids for war. We dare not send them out to public high school and university armed with rubber swords and plastic armor. The time for playing games is past."[3]

It is foolish to think we can prepare our children to change the world for Christ when so little effort is invested in them. Parents who don't prepare their children for the war of ideas raging all around them should not be surprised when their children leave the safety of their homes and the comfort of their youth programs only to abandon Christ and His bride altogether. It is true that equipping and inspiring our children to become fearless defenders of the unborn is only one mark of a mature disciple, but it is a foundational mark to be sure. We are called to raise impassioned disciples of Jesus Christ, marked by a relentless love for God and for others. We do this by teaching them to obey all that Christ commanded.[4] Parents must avoid the depressingly low bar of finding satisfaction in merely raising nice, morally upright young adults. Instead, we must help our young people understand the profundity in Jesus' promise, "If anyone wants to find his life, he must lose it for my sake." With your words and by your example teach your children to "hate what is evil" and "cling to what is good."[5] Help them to recognize the fight against abortion as a good fight to get into. Talk and pray with them about abortion. Take them to an abortion clinic to have their eyes opened and their hearts softened. Connect them with ministries like Project LifeVoice to be trained in pro-life apologetics. Sign them up for a Justice Ride with Created Equal. Doing these things will go a long way in rescuing them from searching for an identity by jumping onto trendy bandwagons. By instilling a vision for life and a commitment to justice in your children, you will drive apathy from their bones and cultivate within their hearts an unbridled love for others so that they will one day valiantly declare, "We didn't pick this fight, but we're going to finish it!"

THE GOSPEL AND THE GIVING OF
OURSELVES

During a visit to the Holocaust Museum in Washington D.C., pro-life author Hadley Arkes and a friend entered a room that housed a large vat filled with the shoes of Jewish victims that had been "collected by the Nazis as they sought to extract anything they could use again or sell." Arkes described the experience:

> "And what came flashing back instantly at that moment were those searing lines of Justice McLean, in his dissenting opinion in the Dred Scott case: You may think that the black man is merely chattel, but 'He bears the impress of his Maker and is amenable to the laws of God and man; and he is destined to an endless existence."[1]

I too visited the Holocaust Museum many years ago and I have seen this same vat of shoes. Nevertheless, Arkes' next sentence stunned me when I first read it, "The sufficient measure of things here is that the Nazis looked at their victims and thought that the shoes were the real durables."

What a poverty of the soul to look at fellow image-bearers and see only their shoes.

This is just one reason why I love the gospel. Worldly thinking blinds us, causing us to value others only to the extent that they benefit us, but the gospel empowers us look beyond one's shoes to find a precious creation of Christ destined to an endless existence and worthy of our love and protection.

CASPER THE FRIENDLY GENTILE

Consider the gospel-saturated life of Casper ten Boom, a humble watchmaker best known as the father of Corrie ten Boom. This unassuming man led his family's valiant wartime efforts to rescue European Jews from annihilation. Today, the ten Boom name is synonymous with love, courage, and self-sacrifice.

Born in the Netherlands on May 19, 1859, Casper grew up in a family that was part of the Dutch Reformed Church, which protested Nazi persecution of Jews. Early in his childhood, his parents' strong Christian faith became his as well. As he continued to mature, the gospel continued to define his convictions and deepen his love for God and others. At 18, Casper moved to Amsterdam and was instrumental in starting a work among the poor. But eventually, he returned to Haarlem where he opened a watchmaker shop. In 1884 he married Cornelia Luitingh and together, they had five children. Just as his parents had taught him, Casper and Cornelia taught their children to love all people and to recognize the special place God has in His heart for the Jewish people. Cornelia died in 1921 and Casper remained faithful to his Christian convictions.

Above Casper's watch shop was his home, where he lived with his two unmarried daughters, Corrie, and Betsie. He was in his eighties when Germany invaded the Netherlands. When the Nazis forced Jews to wear the yellow Star of David on their armbands, Casper decided to wear one too to share in the suffering of his Jewish friends and neighbors. However, his children convinced him not to do so and instead to use their shop and home as cover to rescue Jews. Together, they transformed an upstairs bedroom into a hiding place by bricking in a wall three feet out from the existing wall with a built-in linen pantry through which the Jews could escape into the tiny cavity hidden behind the wall during times of danger.

For many months Casper and his daughters harbored as many as six Jews in their home at a time. However, on February 28, 1944, their home was raided. The Gestapo ransacked the house searching for the Jews but could not find them. They arrested Casper, together with Corrie, Betsie, Willem, and grandson Peter, and took them to the Scheveningen prison camp. Shortly after their arrival, Casper was interrogated. Because of his age, the Gestapo offered to release him to die in the comfort of his own bed if he would tell them where the Jews were hiding and promise to stop his unlawful activities. Despite the danger to his own life, his courageous answer came easily; "If I go home today, tomorrow I will open my door to anyone who knocks for help." When asked if he knew he could die for helping Jews, he stated, "I would consider that the greatest honor that could come to my family." That is precisely what happened; Casper died nine days later, March 9, 1944, at the Hague Municipal Hospital, at the age of 84. There is no retiring from the gospel.

Years later, reflecting on that first night at the Scheveningen prison, Casper's grandson Peter, recalls the emotional agony of that moment and his grandfather's last recorded words:

"Where was the host of angels we had prayed for so often? Had God forgotten us? Then I glanced over at Grandfather sitting in the corner. There was such an expression of peace on his pale face that I could not help marveling. He actually was protected. God had built a fence around him. Suddenly I knew: The everlasting arms are around all of us. God does not make mistakes. He is at the controls.

At last, they took me to my cell. As I walked past Grandfather, I stopped, bent over him, and kissed him goodbye. He looked up at me and said, 'My boy, are we not a privileged generation?'

Those were his last words to me."[2]

THE REAL DURABLES

The Nazi dream of a blonde-haired, blue-eyed, "racially pure" master race would never come about with Casper's help because the gospel rendered him blind to such superficial attributes. Whereas the Nazis looked into the eyes of their Jewish victims and saw nothing of value, Casper saw the real durables. He was firmly convinced that every human being is divinely woven together in the secret place, the womb, and that each of us–regardless of skin color, gender, intelligence, disability, or social standing–has been infused with divine purpose and worth. Casper would have heartily agreed with C.S. Lewis who wrote, "There are no ordinary people. You have never talked to a mere mortal."[3]

But evil regimes are not the only ones that suffer from impaired moral vision. Sometimes the image of God is difficult to recognize in our own lives and in the lives of others. God's designs often appear hazy because of the unremitting effects of the Fall. For example, when a sonogram image reveals a severe fetal abnormality, when tragedy strikes a young athlete with quadriplegia, or when Alzheimer's disease claims the mind of an aging parent, God's divine purposes can seem less than divine. Because we live under the curse, we humans are often a source of tremendous pain and trouble for one another. At times, our physical, emotional, and spiritual needs can become a crushing burden for our loved ones. In addition, we have quirks and personalities that can cause the patience of family and friends to wear thin. For these reasons and more, loving humans can be dreadfully inconvenient, and sometimes terrifying.

Casper certainly found this to be true in Haarlem in 1944. But "perfect love drives out fear,"[4] so when others–even thousands of professing Christians–closed their hearts and their doors to their Jewish neighbors, Casper and his family opened theirs. Rather than retreat to safety, they willingly risked their own lives to obey the two greatest commandments: "Love the Lord your God with all your heart and with all your soul and with all your mind," and, "Love your neighbor as yourself."[5]

REACHING BEYOND OURSELVES

This is the power of the gospel in a believer's life; to be able to clearly see God's divine reflection in the hunted Jew and in the hunted embryo, and to reach beyond our selfish hearts to find the courage to love those who are most unpopular and most inconvenient to love.

The splendor of the Incarnation is that God became flesh and entered into our pain and suffering with us. "God made him who had no sin to be sin for us, so that in him we might become the right-eousness of God."[6] Through His death and Resurrection, Jesus "gave himself as a ransom for all people"[7] and thereby satisfied our Heavenly Father's demand for justice. The gospel is the story of rescue. He became like us so that we might become like Him.

The surprising gift of the gospel is the discovery that real life is found in the giving of ourselves for others. Dying to self is the pathway to a deeper relationship with Christ, a greater love for one another, and a more mature character. Whereas the pro-choice position demands, "Others must die so I can live," Christ taught the opposite; *we must die so others can live*. Jesus told His disciples, "Greater love has no one than this: to lay down one's life for one's friends."[8]

There are no disposable people. We are each a part of God's plan to sanctify, or mature, one another. Although it may have appeared otherwise, Casper needed his Jewish fugitives as much as they needed him. These inconvenient houseguests were part of God's plan to "conform" Casper and his family "to the image of his Son."[9] God uses the neediness of others to grow us into the people He intends for us to become. It is not just that we need others when we are needy; we need the *neediness of others* because we were created to give ourselves away. The unborn child diagnosed with Down syndrome and the aging parent whose mind has been ravaged by Alzheimer's need us, and we need them too. Seemingly impossible circumstances provide opportunities to become more than we ever thought possible. God uses the imperfections of others to perfect us. Even the most severe suffering can have a redemptive effect in our lives and in the lives of those we love.

A PRIVILEGED GENERATION

Casper's rhetorical question, "are we not a privileged generation?", asked while under arrest and threat of execution is lunacy to those who see only shoes, and not the precious image-bearers who wear them. After all, why trouble oneself or risk losing one's own life for strangers, especially for those castigated as "vermin"?

Likewise, many of our own brothers and sisters in Christ question the wisdom of those of us who devote time and energy to giving voice to embryos and fetuses. This is not surprising. After all, when humans are viewed even within many of our churches as only instrumentally valuable and not intrinsically valuable, the loathsome acts of aborting one's offspring or euthanizing one's ailing parent are easily relabeled "reproductive justice" and "death with dignity" and sold as acts of mercy. Those who oppose such "compassion" are often perceived as fanatical. But regardless of how these acts are marketed, they remain acts of supreme selfishness. Innocent human life is never ours to take; it is only ours to cherish and protect. Peter J. Colosi, associate professor of philosophy at Salve Regina University, writes:

> "It's very important to point out that while the love you have for someone is one reason why you would never kill him, it isn't the deepest reason. The deepest reason is the inner worth of the person. Your love for him is inside of you, but his humanity, uniqueness, and preciousness are inside of him."[10]

Colosi makes an excellent point. Not only is the inner worth of an unborn child the deepest reason we should not abort her, but it should also serve as the main reason we should do whatever we can to rescue her from being aborted.

Yes, we too are a privileged generation. This is our time to stand against genocide. Our unborn neighbors are worthy of a robust defense and we are richly blessed to be able to provide it. This is no time for cowardice or apathy. Whatever price we might pay for the grand privilege of rescuing the unborn from abortion will surely prove trivial when the veil of our earthly lives has finally been lifted.

Casper took his Holocaust seriously. May God help us to do the same.

APPENDIX
RESOURCES FOR PRO-LIFE AMBASSADORS

PRO-LIFE BOOKS

The Case for Life: Equipping Christians to Engage the Culture
   Scott Klusendorf, Crossway Books, 2009

Pro-Life Answers to Pro-Choice Arguments
   Randy Alcorn, Multnomah Books, 1992

Defending Life: A Moral and Legal Case Against Abortion Choice
   Francis Beckwith, Cambridge University, 2007

The Ethics of Abortion: Women's Rights, Human Life, and the Question of Justice
   Christopher Kaczor, Routledge, 2011

Seeing Is Believing: Why Our Culture Must Face the Victims of Abortion
Jonathon Van Maren, Life Cycle Books, 2017

Love Thy Body: Answering Hard Questions About Life and Sexuality
Nancy Pearcey, Baker Books, 2018

Tactics: A Game Plan for Discussing Your Christian Convictions
Gregory Koukl, Zondervan, 2009

Shattered into Beautiful: Delivering the Brokenhearted from Abortion
Jeannie Scott Smith, Prose Press, 2011

PRO-LIFE ORGANIZATIONS

Project LifeVoice, www.projectlifevoice.com

Created Equal, www.createdequal.org

Life Training Institute, www.prolifetraining.com

Stand to Reason, www.str.org

Heartbeat International, www.heartbeatinternational.org

LIFESITE News, www.lifesitenews.com

Canadian Centre for Bio-Ethical Reform, www.endthekilling.ca

ENDNOTES

OUR MANSLOW MOMENT

1. Manslow was not his real name.

1. EVERYONE HAS A BACKSTORY

1. Matthew 12:37
2. *The Silent Scream,* American Portrait Films, 1984
3. 1 Peter 5:1
4. Matt 11:28-29
5. Jude 22
6. Dietrich Bonhoeffer, "The Church and the Jewish Question," in No Rusty Swords: Letters, Lectures and Notes 1928-1936 (New York: Harper and Row, 1965), 225

2. RESCUERS, REFORMERS, AND CAGE-RATTLERS

1. G.K. Chesterton, *Heretics*, (London: The Bodley Head, 1905), 61
2. Ephesians 5:25
3. Philippians 2:8
4. John 15:18
5. Matthew 16:13-18
6. This paragraph is not offered as a statement about pacifism. The role of the corporate Church is distinct from the role of individual Christians, many of whom feel biblically justified to participate in just wars, to serve in the military, etc.
7. John 15:15
8. Barna Group, "5 Things You Need to Know About Adoption", November 4, 2013, https://www.barna.com/research/5-things-you-need-to-know-about-adoption/
9. Phillips Verner Bradford and Harvey Blume, *Ota Benga: The Pygmy in the Zoo*, (New York: St. Martin's Press, 1992), 183
10. Philip Hallie, *Lest Innocent Blood Be Shed*, (New York: HarperPerennial, 1979), 108
11. 1 John 4:19

12. Judicial Watch, "Federal Court Slams Potentially Illicit Sales of Body Parts of Aborted Fetuses–Orders Release of Additional Information on Organ Purchases", March 15, 2021, https://www.judicialwatch.org/press-releases/aborted-fetuses-information/

3. WHAT IS THE ZYGOTE AND WHY DOES IT MATTER?

1. Harry Blackmun, *Roe v. Wade*, 410 U.S. 113 (1973)
2. Anthony Kennedy, *Planned Parenthood v. Casey*, 505 U.S. 833 (1992)
3. Cecile Richards, "Planned Politics: Is There a Place for Planned Parenthood in Politics?" interview with Jorge Ramos, America with Jorge Ramos, Fusion TV, February 27, 2014, 00:58, https://www.youtube.com/watch?v=ZdK--xwxwBA
4. Dr. C. Ward Kischer, "Why Hatch is Wrong on Human Life", Human Events, July 16, 2001, http://www.lifeissues.net/writers/kisc/kisc_06whywrong.html
5. Keith Moore, TVN Persaud, Mark Torchia, *The Developing Human: Clinically Oriented Embryology,* 9th edition, (Saunders, 2011), 2
6. Steve Jacobs, "Balancing Abortion Rights and Fetal Rights: A Mixed Mediation of the U.S. Abortion Debate", (Ph.D., diss., University of Chicago, 2019), 255
7. Tony Campolo, *Stories That Feed Your Soul*, (Ventura, California: Regal, 2010), 156
8. Robert George, "A Distinct Human Organism", NPR, November 22, 2005, https://www.npr.org/templates/story/story.php?storyId=4857703
9. Maureen Condic, *"Life: Defining the Beginning by The End",* First Things, May 2003, https://www.firstthings.com/article/2003/05/life-defining-the-beginning-by-the-end
10. Blastocyst is the scientific term to refer to the developing prenatal human being at day five or six
11. Patrick Lee and Robert George, "Silver Lining," National Review, October 19, 2006, https://www.nationalreview.com/2006/10/silver-lining-patrick-lee-robert-p-george/
12. Randy Alcorn, *Why Pro-Life? Caring for the Unborn and Their Mothers*, (Sandy, Oregon: Eternal Perspectives Ministries, 2012), 33
13. Jerome LeJeune, *The Concentration Can*, (California: Ignatius Press, 1992), 11
14. Scott Klusendorf, *The Case for Life*, (Illinois: Crossway Books, 2009), 35
15. Peter Singer, *Practical Ethics*, (New York: Cambridge University Press, 2011), 85-86
16. Francis Beckwith, *"Understanding the Abortion Debate,"* The Summit Lecture Series, www.summit.org
17. Fr. Richard John Neuhaus, foreword to Maureen Condic's article, *"When Does Human Life Begin? A Scientific Perspective",* The Catholic Bioethics Quarterly, Vol. 9, Issue 1, Spring 2009, https://doi.org/10.5840/ncbq20099184

4. WHAT IF SUSAN COULDN'T SING?

1. Portions of this chapter were originally published for *Life Training Institute* and later in *Christian Research Journal*, (Vol. 37 No.6, 2014) in my article titled, "What If Susan Couldn't Sing? Identifying and Avoiding Bad Pro-life Arguments."

2. Piers Morgan, *Britain's Got Talent*, April 11, 2009, Episode 1

3. Simon Cowell, *Britain's Got Talent*, April 11, 2009, Episode 1

4. This expression originated in the Bible (Matthew 23:24) and refers to criticizing others for minor or inconsequential offenses while ignoring or overlooking offenses of much greater weight or concern.

5. Christopher Kazcor, *The Ethics of Abortion*, (New York: Routledge, 2001), 93

6. Pro-life people also acknowledge a distinction between humanness and personhood (e.g. angels are persons but are not humans). But according to the endowment view of persons, one's personhood depends on what one is rather than the functions one performs. This means all human beings are persons, deserving of respect as persons, because all human beings have the same nature throughout their entire life.

7. Peter Singer, *Practical Ethics*, (New York: Cambridge University Press, 2000), 160-161

8. Singer, *Practical Ethics*, 185

9. Nat Hentoff, "A Professor Who Argues for Infanticide", *The Washington Post*, September 11, 1999, https://www.washingtonpost.com/archive/opinions/1999/09/11/a-professor-who-argues-for-infanticide/cce7dc81-3775-4ef6-bfea-74cd795fc43f/

10. Nancy Pearcey, *Love Thy Body*, (Michigan: Baker Books, 2018), 57

11. Many pro-choice philosophers recognize that traits such as self-awareness come in varying degrees but argue there is a threshold one must pass to be considered a person. Accordingly, everyone who passes that threshold is a person, regardless of how much they differ from others in that function. However, as Christopher Kaczor writes, "performance-threshold accounts of personhood can establish that two normal adults both count as persons, but given human inequalities in degreed qualities (self-awareness, etc.), such accounts cannot establish that any two individual adults have equal moral worth as persons, and hence equal rights," *The Ethics of Abortion*, (New York: Routledge, 2001), 103

12. Christopher Kaczor, *The Ethics of Abortion*, (New York: Routledge, 2001), 93

13. Pearcey, *Love Thy Body*, 59

14. Roger B. Taney, *Dred Scott v. Sandford*, 60 U.S. (19 How.) 393 (1857)

15. John Stonestreet, *The Victims of Bad Ideas*, Breakpoint Colson Center, May 3, 2019, 00:17, https://www.breakpoint.org/bp-this-week-the-victims-of-bad-ideas/

16. Christopher Kaczor, *The Ethics of Abortion*, (New York: Routledge, 2001), 93

17. Thomas Jefferson, The Declaration of Independence (US 1776)

18. Clinton Wilcox, Facebook post, 2018

19. Joseph Sobran, *The Cost of Abortion*, October 27, 1998

20. Jay Watts, President, Merely Human Ministries, Facebook post, 2016

21. Intrinsic value is a property of anything that is valuable on its own. In contrast, instrumental value is a property of anything that derives its value from a relation to another.

22. Tanya Gold, *"It wasn't singer Susan Boyle who was ugly on Britain's Got Talent so much as our reaction to her"*, The Guardian, April 15, 2009, https://www.theguardian.com/commentisfree/2009/apr/16/britains-got-talent-susan-boyle

23. John 13:35

5. MISSING PERSONS

1. Exodus 1:15-22

2. Matthew 2:16

3. Jill Filipovic, "Yes, Let's Be Honest About Kermit Gosnell's Abortion 'House of Horrors'", The Guardian, 2013, https://www.theguardian.com/commentisfree/2013/apr/19/gosnell-abortion-trial-pro-life-activists-to-blame

4. Associated Press, "Final Arguments in Gosnell Trial", *Politico*, April 29, 2013, https://www.politico.com/story/2013/04/kermit-gosnell-abortion-closing-arguments-090753

5. Kirsten Powers, "Philadelphia Abortion Clinic Horror", *USA Today*, April 11, 2013, https://www.usatoday.com/story/opinion/2013/04/10/philadelphia-abortion-clinic-horror-column/2072577/

6. Cathie Humbarger, "2,246 Fetal Remains Found at Abortionist's Home Should be the Catalyst to End Abortion," *The Federalist*, September 18, 2019, https://thefederalist.com/2019/09/18/fetal-remains-on-george-klopfer-property-catalyst-to-end-abortion/

7. Romans 1:30

8. Willie Parker, *Life's Work: A Moral Argument for Choice*, (New York: Atria Books, 2017), 5

9. Ibid.

10. Parker, *Life's Work: A Moral Argument for Choice*, 13

11. Parker, *Life's Work: A Moral Argument for Choice*, 95

12. Ibid., 95-96

13. Frederick Douglass, *My Bondage, My Freedom*, (Toronto, Canada: Dover Publications, Inc., 1969), 65

14. Gregg Cunningham, "Debate on Graphic Abortion Images", *AbortionNo.org*, April 17, 2014, 54:32, https://www.abortionno.org/videogallery/debate-on-graphic-abortion-images/

15. Tom O'Neill, Visions on Earth, *National Geographic*, The Photo Issue, October 2013, 37

16. Ibid, p. 135

17. Gregg Cunningham, "Debate on Graphic Abortion Images", *AbortionNo.org*, April 17, 2014, 23:33, https://www.abortionno.org/videogallery/debate-on-graphic-abortion-images/

18. Naomi Wolf, *"Our Bodies, Our Souls: Rethinking Prochoice Rhetoric,"* The New Republic, 1995, Oct. 16, 213 (16).

19. Ibid.

20. Jonathan Van Maren, *Seeing Is Believing*, (Toronto, Ontario: Life Cycle Books, 2017), 84

6. AMERICA'S FORCED ABORTION POLICY

1. Planned Parenthood, "Planned Parenthood Statement in Support of Chen Guangcheng Denounces Coercive Reproductive Health Policies in China," January 30, 2014, https://www.plannedparenthood.org/about-us/newsroom/press-releases/planned-parenthood-statement-support-chen-guangcheng-denounces-coercive-reproductive-health-pol

2. Nancy Flanders, "China Continues Population Control, Even Under New '3-Child' Policy", *WorldNetDaily.com*, June 5, 2021, https://www.wnd.com/2021/06/china-continues-population-control-even-new-3-child-policy/

3. Greg Koukl, "I'm Pro-Choice", *Stand to Reason*, April 2, 2013, https://www.str.org/w/i-m-pro-choice

4. Bernard Nathanson and Richard Ostling, *Aborting America*, (New York: Pinnacle Books, 1979), 197

5. Mary Calderone, "Illegal Abortion as a Public Health Problem", *American Journal of Public Health*, Volume 50, no. 7, (July 1960): 949

6. Lisa M. Koonin, et al, "Abortion Surveillance -- United States, 1992", *Center for Disease Control and Prevention*, https://www.cdc.gov/mmwr/preview/mmwrhtml/00041486.htm

7. Wesley J. Smith, "Pro-Lifers: Get Out of Medicine!", *First Things*, May 12, 2017, https://www.firstthings.com/web-exclusives/2017/05/pro-lifers-get-out-of-medicine

8. Marist Poll, "America's Opinions on Abortion", Knights of Columbus, January 2021, https://www.kofc.org/en/resources/news-room/polls/kofc-americans-opinions-on-abortion012021.pdf

9. Kyle Blanchette, "No, Pro-Lifers Are Not Merely Pro-Birth", *Washington Examiner*, May 25, 2019, https://www.washingtonexaminer.com/opinion/op-eds/no-pro-lifers-are-not-merely-pro-birth

10. Marc Newman, Facebook Post, November 23, 2016

11. Francis J. Beckwith, Facebook post, 2018

12. Alcorn, *Pro-Life vs. Pro-Choice*, EPM, 107

13. Jennifer Granholm, "The War Room with Jennifer Granholm", *Current TV*, (this video is no longer available on-line but is in the author's possession)
14. This number includes approximately 450 surgical abortion clinics and 250 chemical abortion clinics. Operation Rescue, January 7, 2021, https://www.operationrescue.org/archives/the-status-of-american-abortion-facilities-in-2020-the-first-abortion-free-state/

7. "MY NAME IS IDIOT"

1. Joseph Fletcher, "The Pursuit of Happiness: Being Happy, Being Human," *The Humanist 35*, no. 1 (January 1975), 47-58, as republished in Humanhood.
2. Larry Lader, "The Abortion Revolution." *The Humanist*, May/June 1973, 4
3. Children's Defense Fund, "The State of America's Children 2020", https://www.childrensdefense.org/the-state-of-americas-children-2020/ (accessed April 2021)
4. Edward Thatch, *"6 Reasons Why We Should Support Abortion,"* March 29, 2013, www.returnofkings.com
5. International Planned Parenthood Federation website, "Abortion: The Right to Choose Is a Human Right," September 27, 2013
6. Lila Rose, "The Myth of Empowerment Through Abortion," *The Washington Times*, June 3, 2013, https://www.washingtontimes.com/news/2013/jun/3/the-myth-of-empowerment-through-abortion/
7. Jeffrey Ventrella, Alliance Defending Freedom. Mr. Ventrella had shared this statement in various public speaking events.
8. Matthew 11:28-29
9. The Turnaway Study, Advancing New Standards in Reproductive Health (ANSIRH), 2008
10. Planned Parenthood, https://www.plannedparenthood.org/learn/abortion/in-clinic-abortion-procedures/how-safe-is-an-in-clinic-abortion (assessed July, 2021)
11. Priscilla K. Coleman, "Abortion and Mental Health", *The British Journal of Psychiatry*, Volume 199, Issue 3, September 2011, 180 - 186
12. Mika Gissler, Elina Hemminki, Jouko Lonnqvist, "Suicides After Pregnancy in Finland: 1987-94: Register Linkage Study", *British Medical Journal* 313:1431-4, 1996
13. U.S. Food & Drug Administration, Questions and Answers on Mifeprex, www.fda.gov, April 12, 2019, https://www.fda.gov/drugs/postmarket-drug-safety-information-patients-and-providers/questions-and-answers-mifeprex
14. John Newton, *Thoughts Upon the African Slave Trade*, London, Printed for J. Buckland, In Pater-Noster-Row; And J. Johnson, In St. Paul's Church-Yard, 1788, 14
15. Warren Hern, M.D, and Billie Corrigan, R.N., *"What About Us? Staff Reactions to D & E"*, 1980, 7
16. Debra Nucatola, Senior Director of Medical Services of Planned Parenthood,

Alliance Defending Freedom, 2015, 01:25, https://www.youtube.com/watch?v=wnLfGWbmh3g,

17. Frederick Douglass, Speech at Civil Rights Mass Meeting, Washington, D.C. (October 22, 1883)

18. Charitie Lees Bancroft, *Before the Throne of God Above*, (originally titled, *The Advocate*), 1863, public domain

8. THE ONES WE'RE ASHAMED OF

1. Greg Koukl, "Why Abortion Is a Yawner", July 08, 2005, https://str.typepad.com/weblog/2005/07/why_abortion_is_1.html

2. Pearcey, *Love Thy Body*, 56

3. *The Count of Monte Cristo*, directed by Kevin Reynolds, (Buena Vista Pictures, 2002), DVD

4. Hadley Arkes, *Natural Rights and the Right to Choose*, (New York: Cambridge University Press, 2002), 2

5. Matthew 25:40

9. DID GOD REALLY SAY THAT?

1. Pro-abortion philosopher Judith Jarvis Thomson likens the unborn child to an intruder and makes the outlandish claim that just because a woman consents to sex does not mean she consents to pregnancy. She asks us to imagine "people seeds" that fly through the air. Suppose one makes its way through your window screen and nests in your carpet where it will continue to develop into a person for whom you will be responsible. Thomson concludes that just as you are under no moral obligation to allow people seeds to live and grow in your home, a pregnant woman has no moral duty to loan her uterus to a fetus that was conceived from using failed contraceptives.

2. Whoopi Goldberg, *The View*, aired September 22nd, 2015

3. Pete Buttigieg, "The Generous Gospel of Mayor Pete", *Rolling Stone Magazine,* as interviewed by Alex Morris, November 20, 2019

4. Isaiah 7:14

5. John 1:14

6. Luke 1:41

7. Luke 1:44

8. Exodus 20:13

9. Leviticus 18:21

10. Leviticus 20:2

11. Leviticus 20:4-5

12. Exodus 21:22-24, Revised Standard Version
13. See Genesis 1:24; 8:17; 15:4; 25:26; 1 Kings 8:19 and 2 Kings 20:18
14. Genesis 3:1
15. 2 Peter 3:16
16. Isaiah 5:20

10. OBSTACLES, HURDLES, AND HITCHES

1. Acts 4:19
2. Michael Horton, *Beyond Culture Wars*, (Chicago: Moody Press, 1994), 59
3. Psalm 33:16-22
4. Abraham Kuyper, *Sphere Sovereignty*, The Free University, October 20, 1880
5. Ephesians 1:22
6. Revelation 19:16, KJV
7. Proverbs 24:11
8. Margaret Anderson and Patricia Collins, *Race, Class & Gender: Intersections and Inequalities,* (Independence, Kentucky: Cengage Learning Publishers, 2019), 5
9. Francis Beckwith, "Abortion and Rape: Answering the Arguments for Abortion Rights", CRI, March 26, 2009, https://www.equip.org/article/abortion-and-rape-answering-the-arguments-for-abortion-rights/
10. Martin Gansberg, *"Thirty-Eight Who Saw Murder Didn't Call the Police,"* *The New York Times*, March 27, 1964, https://www.nytimes.com/1964/03/27/archives/37-who-saw-murder-didnt-call-the-police-apathy-at-stabbing-of.html
11. Romans 3:20
12. Stephanie Gray Connors, "Love Unleashes Life", Westside Church sermon, January 20, 2017, 07:04, https://www.youtube.com/watch?v=FwIhCQC8qgs&t=442s
13. Horatio Gates Spafford, *It Is Well with My Soul*, Gospel Hymns No. 2 by Ira Sankey and Bliss (1876), public domain.
14. Randy Alcorn, "William Carey: The Father of Modern Missions was a Prolife Activist," Eternal Perspectives Ministries, October 26, 2016, https://www.ep-m.org/blog/2016/Oct/26/william-carey-prolife-activist?fbclid=IwAR3R6oBO1cb_j-UZ9uwGFvoPVvYUAtrG5Mu_M_KBgUZ7wKVLHXFKCNOIA3Lo
15. Ephesians 4:15
16. Brian Clowes, "Is the Mainstream Media Really Biased on Abortion?*",* Human Life International, May 17, 2019, www.hli.org, https://www.hli.org/resources/mainline-media-really-biased-abortion/
17. Marc Lamont Hill, "Liberal Commentator: We 'Made a Decision' Not to Cover Gosnell to Protect Abortion," LifeSite News, April 17, 2013, https://www.lifesitenews.com/news/liberal-commentator-the-media-made-a-decision-not-to-cover-gosnell-to-prote/
18. Melinda Henneberger, "Why Kermit Gosnell Hasn't Been on Page One", *The Wash-*

ington Post, April 15, 2013, https://www.washingtonpost.com/blogs/she-the-people/wp/2013/04/15/why-kermit-gosnell-hasnt-been-on-page-one/

19. Susanne Millsaps, executive director of Utah NARAL, quoted in *The Washington Times*, March 13, 1991. Also quoted in *Voices for the Unborn* (Feasterville, Pennsylvania, 1991), 4

20. Jill Filipovic, "A New Poll Shows What Really Interests 'Pro-Lifers': Controlling Women", *The Guardian*, August 22, 2019, https://www.theguardian.com/comment-isfree/2019/aug/22/a-new-poll-shows-what-really-interests-pro-lifers-controlling-women?fbclid=IwAR1UyzrmUtVRoOHddpO3K8uSw-oMjIHvaUkUml4MBSu8r-RUMSxQHOjsApQ0

21. James 4:17

11. UNMUTING THE PULPIT

1. John 10:12-13, NKJV
2. Ezekiel 34:1-2
3. Jude 12
4. Gregg Cunningham, as quoted by Scott Klusendorf, *The Case for Life,* (Illinois: Crossway Books, 2009), 10
5. James 5:16
6. Ephesians 6:18
7. Richard Dawkins, *The Selfish Gene*, Preface to First Edition, (New York: Oxford University Press, 1976, 1989)
8. Lawrence Krauss, as quoted by Richard Panek, "Out There," *New York Times*, March 11, 2007, https://www.nytimes.com/2007/03/11/magazine/11dark.t.html
9. Camille Paglia, *Vamps & Tramps*, (New York: Vintage Books, 1994), 71
10. Peter Singer explains, "The belief that mere membership of our species, irrespective of other characteristics, makes a great difference to the wrongness of killing a being is a legacy of religious doctrines," *Practical Ethics*, (New York: Cambridge University Press, 1993), 150
11. William Lane Craig, *On Guard: Defending Your Faith with Reason and Precision*, (Colorado: David C. Cook, 2010), 18
12. Proverbs 31:8
13. Acts 20:27
14. 2 Corinthians 5:16
15. Matthew 25:40
16. Ezekiel 2:5
17. Frederick Douglass, *My Bondage and My Freedom,* (Toronto, Ontario: Dover Publications, 1969), 445
18. Ephesians 4:15
19. John 8:36

20. 2 Corinthians 7:10
21. Scott Klusendorf, *The Case for Life*, (Illinois: Crossway Books, 2009), 212
22. 2 Timothy 1:7

12. THE ART OF ARGUING WELL

1. Colossians 3:5-6
2. John Lennox, "Becoming A Winsome Apologist", Xenos Summer Institute 2013, 16:06, https://www.youtube.com/watch?v=FwOpsOudaA8
3. Psalm 145:8
4. Colossians 3:12
5. 1 Peter 3:15
6. Antonin Scalia, "Interview with Lesley Stahl", *CBS 60 Minutes*, April 27, 2008, 06:46, https://www.youtube.com/watch?v=FrFj7JAyutg
7. 2 Corinthians 5:14
8. 2 Corinthians 10:5-6
9. Matthew 5:46
10. Scott Klusendorf, "*Speaking Up to Defend Life*", Focus on The Family, www.focusonthefamily.com
11. Greg Koukl, "*Only One Question*", *Stand to Reason,* https://www.str.org/w/only-one-question
12. Mark Harrington, "*Why Opposing Abortion Comes at a Cost*", August 7, 2021, 00:33, https://www.youtube.com/watch?v=FLdctuzX0Kk
13. 1 Corinthians 6:20
14. 2 Corinthians 5:20
15. Titus 2:10
16. Proverbs 16:24
17. Luke 6:45

13. RAISING THE RIGHT KIND OF REBELS

1. A 2012 meta-review of 24 studies conducted between 1995 and 2011 found that between 61 percent and 93 percent of U.S. women choose abortion after a Down-syndrome diagnosis, a range the researchers narrowed to a "weighted mean" of 67 percent. Jaime L. Natoli, Deborah L. Ackerman, Suzanne McDermott, Janice G. Edwards, "Prenatal Diagnosis of Down Syndrome: A Systematic Review of Termination Rates", (1995-2011), March 14, 2012
2. Ephesians 2:10
3. William Lane Craig, "Christian Apologetics: Who Needs It?", *Reasonable Faith,*

https://www.reasonablefaith.org/writings/popular-writings/apologetics/christian-apologetics-who-needs-it
4. Matthew 28:19-20
5. Romans 12:9

THE GOSPEL AND THE GIVING OF OURSELVES

1. Hadley Arkes, *Natural Rights & the Right to Choose*, (New York: Cambridge University Press, 2002), 1
2. Corrie ten Boom, *Father ten Boom*, (New Jersey: Fleming H. Revell Company, 1978), 10-11
3. C.S. Lewis, *The Weight of Glory*, (New York: HarperOne, 2001), 45-46
4. 1 John 4:18, NKJV
5. Matthew 22:37-38
6. 2 Corinthians 5:21
7. 1 Timothy 2:6
8. John 15:13
9. Romans 8:29
10. Peter J. Colosi, "What's Love Got to Do with It? The Ethical Contradictions of Peter Singer", *Catholic Education Resource Center*, https://www.catholiceducation.org/en/health/euthanasia-and-assisted-suicide/what-s-love-got-to-do-with-it-the-ethical-contradictions-of-peter-singer.html

ACKNOWLEDGMENTS

I want to acknowledge several people for their influence and support in my pro-life work. Thank you to my friend, Joe Jacobs, for first exposing me to abortion's primary victims in 1984. God used you to set me on this course.

My deepest gratitude as well to pastor Wendell Brane for your example of courageous pastoral leadership and sacrificial love for the unborn. Thank you to Scott Klusendorf; being associated with your good name while serving on the teaching staff of Life Training Institute opened many doors of ministry for me.

I would like to recognize my daughter and son-in-law, Aubrie and Seth Drayer, my friends, Pat Schwenk, David Warbington, Clinton Wilcox, Lisa Cerasoli, and my pastors, Shawn Meyer and Phil Bange, who offered many suggestions to various sections of my manuscript.

Thank you to my editor, Marcus Costantino, and to Dave Sheets, president of Believer's Books Services. Whatever errors of commission or omission appear in these pages are mine and mine alone.

A special debt of gratitude is owed to my faithful ministry partners who continue to invest their prayers and treasure in my work. Because of you, children are being rescued from abortion, and men and women who have been responsible for abortions are finding Christ's forgiveness and healing.

Thank you to my parents, Don and Lee Spencer, whose love for the outcast and the oppressed have made an indelible impression on me. Thank you to my children, Aubrie, Marisa, Summer, Ian, and Katerine. You have enriched my life beyond measure. And to my wife, Barbara, to whom this book is dedicated; every day with you is a joy.

Finally, and most importantly, I thank my Heavenly Father who rescued me from darkness and brought me into the Kingdom of the Son He loves.

ABOUT THE AUTHOR

Michael Spencer served as a pastor for 23 years and now serves as the founder and president of Project Life-Voice, a gospel-driven human rights organization that equips and inspires pro-life ambassadors to speak compellingly and to act sacrificially on behalf of our unborn neighbors.

He travels extensively throughout the United States and beyond, speaking in churches, at banquets and conferences, and on high school and university campuses. Michael brings a pastor's heart to the often emotional and divisive issue of abortion in a way that is both gracious and compelling.

To find out more about Michael or Project LifeVoice, visit www.projectlifevoice.com.